TO MAKE A DIFFERENCE

To Make a Difference

A Prescription for a Good Life

Morris Goodman

with Joel Yanofsky

Published for Pharmascience Inc.
by
McGill-Queen's University Press
Montreal & Kingston · London · Ithaca

ISBN 978-0-7735-4334-8 (cloth)
ISBN 978-0-7735-9044-1 (ePDF)
ISBN 978-0-7735-9045-8 (ePUB)

Legal deposit second quarter 2014
Bibliotheque nationale du Québec

Printed in Canada on acid-free paper that is 100% ancient forest free
(100% post-consumer recycled), processed chlorine free.

McGill-Queen's University Press acknowledges the support of the
Canada Council for the Arts for our publishing program. We also
acknowledge the financial support of the Government of Canada
through the Canada Book Fund for our publishing activities.

Library and Archives Canada Cataloguing in Publication

Goodman, Morris, 1931 –, author
     To make a difference : a prescription for a good life / Morris Goodman
with Joel Yanofsky.

Issued in print and electronic formats.
ISBN 978-0-7735-4334-8 (bound). – ISBN 978-0-7735-9044-1 (ePDF). –
ISBN 978-0-7735-9045-8 (ePUB)

     1. Goodman, Morris, 1931 –. 2. Businesspeople – Québec (Province) –
Montréal – Biography. 3. Pharmacists – Québec (Province) – Montréal –
Biography. 4. Philanthropists – Québec (Province) – Montréal – Biography.
5. Ukrainian Canadians – Québec (Province) – Montréal – Biography.
6. Jews – Québec (Province) – Montréal – Biography. 7. Pharmaceutical
industry – Québec (Province) – Montréal – History. 8. Success in business –
Québec (Province) – Montréal – Biography. 9. Success – Québec (Province)–
Montréal – Biography. 10. Montréal (Québec) – Biography. I. Yanofsky, Joel,
1955 –, author II. Title.

HD9670.C32G65 2014   338.7'61615092   C2014-900688-8
                                          C2014-900689-6

Typeset by MIC 10.5/13 Sabon

In recognition of the sacrifices my parents made
for me and my sisters, Jenny and Luba.

And for my wife, Roz, with love.

Contents

TO MAKE A DIFFERENCE

The purpose of life ... is, above all, to matter,
to count, to stand for something, to have made
some difference that you lived at all.
Leo Rosten

Prologue

Each of us is an author, writing, with deeds.
Mahzor Hadash

Why write my memoirs? There are many reasons, of course, but the most important is the opportunity to leave a record for my family and for future generations who may, as a result, be able to understand a little better what it was like to live in this particular place at this particular time. Wanting to leave such an account is motivated, I suspect, by the fact that my knowledge of my family's past goes back only two generations, and that just barely. I only knew one grandparent, my father's father, and, as we lived in different cities, I did not get to know him well. Whatever stories he might have been able to share with me about himself and his parents and grandparents are lost forever.

There are times I find myself wishing that the wisdom of the generations that have come before us could somehow be transmitted at birth, as part of our genetic blueprint. But since, instead, each generation has to relearn the lessons of the past, I have always believed in the essential role education plays in all our lives. I hope this book will serve as an educational resource for future generations. I hope, too, that by chronicling my life, with its inevitable ups and downs, challenges and achievements, I will be able to convey many of the lessons I have learned.

First and foremost, though, *To Make a Difference* is an expression of enduring gratitude, intended for the people who have made possible, in one way and another, the life I have been lucky enough to live. It is my way of thanking the long list of men and women, role models and mentors, who have generously shared their knowledge, wisdom, and experience with me throughout my life.

The list starts, naturally enough, with my parents, David and Ethel, who taught by example and deed, by their commitment to their children, to hard work, and to their community. This thank-you extends to my sisters, Luba and Jenny, who always supported, and even on occasion spoiled, their younger brother. There were educators too, teachers, like Mr. Stewart at Strathcona Academy, who was dedicated to helping students like me. There were spiritual leaders, like Rabbi Bender of the Adath Israel Congregation, who shared his profound wisdom with young congregants like me. There were community leaders like Joel Sternthal and family members, like my wife Roz's uncle, Dr. David Sherman, whose dedication to medicine was an enormous influence on me. And, of course, there is my wife, Rosalind. I am not a man inclined to gush. Anyone who knows me will tell you I do not wear my heart on my sleeve, but I cannot pass up this opportunity to express my gratitude to my wife of fifty-two years. She has made my life richer than I could have ever imagined and filled it with more companionship and love than any person could hope for. Roz has also never failed to teach me, through her example and deeds, the importance as well as the necessity of philanthropy. She has played a pivotal role in helping build all the businesses I have been involved with over the years. In their own way, my children, Deborah, David, Jonathan, and Shawna, have also taught me more than I can ever convey here about the joys and responsibilities that go hand-in-hand with fatherhood. That would need another book.

And I cannot forget my first real mentor, Manny Winrow, who hired me as a message boy and put me to work in his pharmacy and, in his own uniquely indirect way, gave me a gift for a lifetime – a career I have been able to pursue with passion, curiosity, and commitment. A career I have been able to love.

I have learned an invaluable lesson from all these people and from many more whom you will meet in the following pages; I have learned the joy of helping others. By this, I do not just mean donating money to a cause or a foundation you believe in. While that is one way of providing help, it is not the only way. Often, much more important, is the will required to share with others what you possess – knowledge, experience, stories. In a lifetime of rewards, the satisfaction I have gained from helping empower young people continues to be the greatest reward I have ever received.

This book is also intended to be an expression of my gratitude to Canada, a country I love, which has provided me and my family with freedom and opportunity, a country I fervently hope will continue to offer similar benefits to all its citizens.

◆

Given that I was born just as the Great Depression was beginning and the Second World War was looming, it seems odd to say that the timing was fortuitous. But it was; in fact, it could hardly have been better. Not only was I fortunate that my parents made the difficult, daring decision to come to Canada, but I have been able to witness such great, historic moments as the demise of Hitler in Europe, the birth of modern Israel, the collapse of the Soviet Union, and, of course, the growth of Canada. I came of age at a time in a young country when there were abundant opportunities for a young man with ambition, vision, and a willingness to work tirelessly to make a good life for his family; a young man who was fortunate enough to choose to do a job he has enjoyed thoroughly.

I am a pharmacist by profession and a good deal of my success in the pharmaceutical business is based on my faith in chemistry, in recognizing formulas that work and being willing to undertake the trial and error required to come up with and develop those formulas. It occurs to me, now, that a life succeeds through a similar kind of chemistry – one of trial and error. In my time, I have made many miscalculations. I have followed leads that did not pay off. I have been too impulsive in some decisions, too cautious in others. I relied on people I should not have relied on. I have been pleasantly surprised by others. I have, for the most part, trusted my instincts and, for the most part, my instincts have been right.

A life is also a kind of experiment. We are the sum of our parts, of what we are born with and the experiences we accumulate along the way, of how those parts combine, interact with, and react to one another, how they form a distinct individual.

When I began this project I assumed it would be clearly divided into three sections: family, business, and community. The more I worked on it, however, the more apparent it became that these elements have been, and remain, inextricably intertwined in my life. The challenge, as with a chemical formula, has been to find the precise balance: how to mix a meaningful work life with a rich and happy family life. So, while it is true I am a self-confessed workaholic – and proud of it, by the way – I am proud, too, to be a dedicated husband and father.

I have also worked hard to walk what often seems like a constantly shifting line between being a successful businessman and a caring, compassionate, and happy person. In Yiddish, the word for someone who achieves this state of being is mensch – a word I am particularly fond of. A mensch is a person who has improved not just his own life but the lives of others, a person who has made, and continues to make, a difference in the lives of others. Someone once asked me, "Can a person be both a success in business and a mensch?"

This book and the stories contained in it are intended to answer that question.

The Goodman family: Luba, Jenny, and Morris with their parents, Ethel and David (1934)

Luba Goodman and George Coviensky's wedding, 6 June 1943

Morris and his sister Jenny (1936)

Morris at age thirteen (1944)

Morris's bar mitzvah in October 1944 with his
family and grandfather Joseph Goodman
(bottom left)

The Goodman family in Brooklyn, NY, in 1951

Rabbi Charles Bender

Form 0637A 10M-11-50

In the Superior Court for the Province of Quebec
DISTRICT OF MONTREAL

No.　　　　Vol. *85 PS.*

I, the undersigned, deputy-prothonotary of the said Superior Court for the District of

Montreal, certify that, on *May 2nd* 19 *52*

M r. *Emmanuel L. Weinrauch, druggist*

　　　　　　　　　　　　　　　　　　　of the City of Montreal

has deposited and filed in the office of the Prothonotary of the said Superior

Court, a declaration stating that *he* intend s to carry on business, in

Montreal, under the firm name of " *Winley-Morris Co.* "

Montreal, *May 2nd* 19 *52*.

Paul Pelletier

Deputy-Prothonotary.

Morris' first incorporation (Winley-Morris Company)

Werner Stiefel, Morris Goodman, Morty and Pearl Levy at Ruby Foo's in 1952

Morris's graduation from the University of
Montreal (Faculty of Pharmacy) in May 1953

Allan Schmeltzer, a partner in Winrow's drugstore
on Somerled Ave.

Morris promoting anti-tuberculosis agents across Canada in 1954

Rosalind in 1960, shortly before her engagement
to Morris

Morris in 1960, shortly before his engagement
to Rosalind

I

Second Nature

Do what you can, with what you have, where you are.

Theodore Roosevelt

I was born a twin on 14 September 1931 in Montreal's Royal Victoria Hospital. My brother and I both had life-threatening colitis, but he was believed to have a better chance of surviving. As a consequence, the doctors kept him in the hospital in order to care for him while my parents were told to take me home and make me as comfortable as they could for whatever time I had. In retrospect, I can see that my survival provided my first important lesson in medical science and in life: no one can predict the future. There are no sure things.

My survival against the odds became part of family lore and, growing up, I repeatedly heard stories about how I fought to stay in the world. How, for instance, in our cramped cold-water flat at 5359 St. Dominique Street, in a typical immigrant, working-class neighbourhood, my mother did whatever she could think up, dream up really, to nurse me back to health. My sister Luba, who is nine years my senior, still recalls how our mother would boil water for hot compresses, then apply them to my undersized, frail infant's body. Luba vividly recalls how she would do this day and night. Telling the story some eighty years later, she still could not keep from tearing up:

You were a very sick kid. I always begin to cry when I remember the scene. I can still see our mother standing by the stove with this tiny baby, that's you, Morris, and I remember, in that cold-water flat where we lived, those compresses were barely tepid by the time she applied them to you. I also remember that once you got a little better she was always schlepping you to the Montreal Children's Hospital on the tram. That was a hard time for her, for the whole family.

It was a hard time for a lot of people. The Great Depression had begun in Montreal two years earlier, in the fall of 1929, and it had had a devastating effect. In the next few years unemployment rose as high as thirty-three percent in the city, though it had, as Joe King writes in *Fabled City: Jews of Montreal*, a less dramatic effect on the Jewish population, which was approaching 50,000 at the time. According to King, Jewish unemployment was nine percent, not surprising for a hard-working immigrant community. Even so, there was a sense of desperation. As King writes: "Former executives would take any form of employment at any wage. One woman remembers her father would run errands for ten cents or a quarter."

My parents were not strangers to hard work and sacrifice and making ends meet was a daily struggle. So much so that when my mother learned she was pregnant with twins, my father's aunt and uncle, Esther and Boris Dobrow, offered to take one of the infants, thinking she would be relieved to have one less mouth to feed. Of course she said no.

Fortunately, hard work was second nature to my parents. In this respect, they were no different from an entire generation of immigrants who arrived in the ports of New York or Halifax or Montreal from Eastern Europe at the turn of the twentieth century. They came by the hundreds of thousands, fleeing persecution and pogroms, looking for educational as well as economic opportunities and, not insignificantly, the freedom to live as Jews – a freedom consistently and brutally denied them in the Old World.

By the time my parents made their fateful decision to immigrate from the Ukraine, they were part of a remarkable wave that, as historian Irving Howe writes in *World of Our Fathers*, had already seen "approximately one-third of the East European Jews [leave] their homelands – a migration comparable in modern Jewish history only to the flight from the Spanish Inquisition ... The migration of the East European Jews constituted a spontaneous and collective impulse, perhaps even decision, by a people that had come to recognize the need for new modes and possibilities of life."

The twentieth century has had, as everyone now knows, more than its share of devastating and redemptive moments for the Jewish people. The focus, understandably, has been on the middle of the century – on the great tragedy of the Holocaust and the great triumph of the founding of the State of Israel. But what has often been missing from this epic story of survival and achievement is the contribution made by all those who came to this continent at the turn of the twentieth century to make a better life for themselves and their children. The Yiddish-speaking immigrants headed this way thought of North America as the "golden medina" or the golden land. The decision made by so many poor, disenfranchised people to leave the only homes they had known to settle in a foreign land required remarkable fortitude and courage – a collective conviction, as Irving Howe put it, that it was time to seek out "new modes and possibilities." They knew there had to be something better for them and, more important, for their children and grandchildren. These people, the majority of them poor and hard working, were not only embarking on an extraordinary adventure but setting a heroic example. They not only believed in a better future – they were determined to make it better, no matter the cost.

Canada certainly must have seemed like a "golden medina" to my parents, at least compared to what they were leaving behind in their native Ukraine. My mother and father were both born in the *shtetl* of Lysyanka and may have also lived in Tarashcha, where the earliest known Jewish presence can be traced back to 1765. By the time of the Russian Revolution in 1917, Lysyanka, a small village not far from the city of Kiev, was a frequent target of pogroms by Cossacks. The Cossacks, a form of paramilitary organization in the late days of the Czar and the beginning of the Russian Revolution, had free rein and were greatly and rightfully feared by the Jewish population. In fact, when my mother was a teenage girl she was chased and shot at by a mounted Cossack. A bullet struck her in the neck, but she still managed to flee her assailant, stopping when she could to pat snow on her neck in a desperate attempt to stanch the flow of blood. She was lucky – she found a non-Jewish Ukrainian family who agreed to shelter her. But her scar never vanished and become a constant reminder of the terror left behind in the Old World, of what she had barely survived and of what the implications were, in some places, of being a Jew.

A few years after that near-tragic incident, my mother, Ethel Gorbatyuk, and my father, David Kitaigarotski (our original family name),
were married in Lysyanka and, in 1920, settled in the village of
Zvenyhorodka, in the Cherkasy region of the Ukraine.

Unfortunately, the move did not improve their situation and life
remained as difficult and insecure as before. In 1925, three years after
the birth, on 11 June 1922, of my eldest sister, Luba, my parents decided to leave not only Zvenyhorodka but the Ukraine. They set out
for the New World, a small part of a much larger exodus that saw
nearly half a million Ukrainian Jews immigrate in the years between
1915 and 1931.

My parents' first stop was the Dutch port of Rotterdam, where
they found passage on a relatively new ocean liner called the *Volendam*. There were, not surprisingly, no luxuries for immigrants aboard
the ship. My parents and their fellow Jews were crammed into steer-
age. Just imagine it: hundreds of men, women, and children, all
housed in one large, rocking, unsteady room, sometimes for weeks.
There was no privacy to speak of and only the most minimal access
to bath-rooms. Even by the standards of the time, the conditions were
in-humane. According to the online Gjenvick-Gjønvik archives, "It
is doubtful if anywhere else in the entire civilized world can such vile
and disgraceful treatment of human beings in masses be found as on
the majority of the steamships which carry our immigrants to us."

My parents' only relief from the overcrowded accommodations
was to spend as much time as possible on the deck, in the fresh sea
air. Their intended destination was New York, where my father had
family – his uncle Jacob had settled in the city some years earlier. In
1922, my grandfather Joseph, with my father's younger brother,
Boris, and a cousin, Eva Cherkassky, had immigrated to New York.
Cousin Eva's identity had to be obscured when they landed. She had
to be part of the immediate family to be allowed in and so was listed
as Joseph's daughter and Boris's sister. Immigrants, it is worth pointing out, were not all or always poor, innocent, helpless creatures as
they are often portrayed. They were not above bending the rules to
get around the system. My great uncle Jacob, for instance, saw the
name Goodman on a sign (possibly for Goodman's Matzos, a company founded in 1865) and liked it so much he took it for himself. In
the United States, it was a far simpler moniker than Kitaigarotski. As
he may have told his relatives who were still in the Ukraine, Goodman was a new, hopeful name for a new, hopeful world.

But, as it turned out, my parents' long, arduous journey across the Atlantic Ocean was not going to end with a happy family reunion in New York. New legislative restrictions on immigration to the United States had been enacted in 1924 and my parents were too late, by a matter of weeks, to enter the United States. Instead, my parents and my sister moved on to the *Volendam's* next port of call, Halifax's Pier 21 in Canada. They didn't know if they would be granted admission to enter this new country, a country they had probably never heard of. Like most immigrants, they had no detailed knowledge of the place they were headed for and made no distinction between the United States and Canada. All of it was America, plain and simple. If they were lucky, they had some family to rely on when they landed. If they were unlucky, like my parents, they were left to their own devices. I can only imagine the anxiety they felt, and the stress they endured. When my parents landed in Halifax, they must have been even more unsure about what their dreamed-of future had in store for them. Records of their arrival have my father, David, listed as a merchant, thirty-one, and Russian. My mother is listed as Etel rather than Ethel, twenty-eight, and a housewife. And, for some reason, Luba, called Liba in the records, is listed, at the age of three, as a "scholar." Some scholar – she was still mastering baby talk.

When my parents were told they would be allowed to stay in Canada, they got their first taste of the generosity of this country and, specifically, of Canada's Jewish community. They were greeted on arrival by representatives of Halifax's small Jewish community, who were on hand to welcome and assist them. The story goes that for thirty years a legendary local businessman, Noah Heinish, had never failed to greet Jewish newcomers who arrived in Halifax and give them a five-dollar bill. I don't know if this story is true, but I hope it is. My parents could certainly have used the infusion of cash since another one of their documents states that they arrived on Canadian soil with only $15 to their name. A name they had also decided to change to Goodman by the time they arrived in Montreal.

◆

Seven years later, David and Ethel Goodman were still establishing themselves in Montreal when I was born and somehow managed to survive. My twin brother died in the hospital. I do not know if he was born just before or after me. All I really know of him is his name – Mordecai. My parents did not talk about him when I was growing up, nor did they talk about the heartbreak they must have endured after his death. To be honest, I cannot say I thought about what it meant to be a twin. I was growing up in the Depression and the overriding fact about growing up then was that there was always a lot to do just to get by. In some ways, my family was luckier than most. We always had food on the table and a roof over our heads, at a time when families, unable to pay their rent, would routinely move out, or be tossed out by landlords, in the middle of the night. It was a time when the children in some families had to share one pair of shoes. Often, only one child in a family could go to school at a time and in the classroom children routinely fainted from hunger.

Of course, my sister Luba would tell you, now, that I had something more than just getting by on my mind. According to her, I was "a jumpy kid" from the start. Later on, as I got older, she remembers that I was always up to something, dreaming up some plan or other. "Morris was never short on ideas," Luba still says. "And this, you'll notice, hasn't changed."

I also had a keen sense as a child that I was my parents' consolation. I was not very robust growing up and I suspect the fact that I had come so close to dying must have always been in the back of their minds. I was pampered. How could I not be? To be the baby and the only boy in a Jewish family is a *gantseh megillah* – a big deal. I was also referred to as a *Kaddishele*, which means that, as the only male child, I would serve the crucial role of saying Kaddish, the memorial prayer for my parents when they died. (My parents spoke mainly Yiddish at home and it was my first language. I was called Moishe, my Hebrew name, not Morris. Back then, Yiddish was often referred to as Montreal's "third language.") I was such a "big deal" that I took my place in the family for granted. It was simply my life, particularly since, in addition to my parents, I had two doting older sisters, Luba and Jenny.

Sometimes, it seemed like everything was riding on me. You could call it the weight of expectations. Despite this pressure, I remember being a happy kid. Most of all, I remember always being content in my surroundings. The Great Depression would last throughout most of my early childhood – until the beginning of the Second World War in 1939 – but I cannot say I remember feeling the impact of those hard times. I had everything I wanted or so it always seemed to me. What did I need anyway? What does any kid need? I always got my two-cent ice-cream cone. As for the five-cent sugar cone, well, I got that sometimes, too.

In fact, it was so normal for my family to pamper me that one of my earliest and most vivid memories is of a time when I was not treated with the usual kid gloves. When I was around four I made a trip with my mother to New York to visit my grandfather. Along with his son Boris, he owned a gas station on the corner of Washington Avenue and 125th Street in Harlem. I remember my mother and I were staying at Uncle Boris's house and my mother must have gone out shopping, leaving me in my uncle's care for a little while. But I assumed, as a young child might, that she had left me for good. I must have started to cry. Uncle Boris could not handle this. He had two children of his own by then but I am guessing they were not pampered the way I was or he was not used to taking care of them by himself. Whatever the reason, he finally got so fed up with me that he locked me in a small bedroom. Nobody had ever treated me this way before. This experience, which has stayed with me all these years, was a traumatic one.

Now, it is easy to look back on that incident and others and to think how indulged I was. But I can also see that it did not do me any harm in the long run. Instead, I am convinced it made me a more confident, secure person. It may explain why, for instance, whenever I have had setbacks in my career, I have been able to believe in my ability to survive those setbacks and start all over again. I have never doubted I could be successful the next time around.

This probably also explains why I have always believed you should "spoil" children. My belief in the good it did me formed the basis of how Roz and I would treat our own four children. I know that word, "spoil," is not popular nowadays, so let me explain. What it comes down to, of course, is how you spoil your children. You have to do it the right way. Spoil them, yes, with love and some indulgence. There is, in my experience as a father, no better way. Of course, this should hardly come as a surprise: it is what my parents did. They instilled the right values and reinforced them by example, day by day.

2

Mentors

Who is wise? One who learns from every man.
                    Pirkei Avot

I learned the value of work – and the importance of doing the best I could – by a kind of osmosis, absorbing my parents' example. My mother worked tirelessly running the household while my father worked in the bag business for a man named Hymie Clayman. My father's job consisted mainly of recycling jute and cotton bags. Once he had learned the ropes, he went into business for himself. One of his first suppliers was the Richstone Bakery, a successful Montreal business at the time. After the Richstone bags were emptied of flour or sugar, my father would buy them, scour them – a grueling, dirty procedure – and then sell them to other businesses. Recycling was a way of life then, not a lifestyle choice. There was no choice; there were no disposables, no plastic. Back then, nobody gave a second thought to pollution or the environment. No one had even heard of such things.

My father later found other companies from which he could buy large quantities of bags. By the mid-1930s he was making his rounds in a second-hand black pickup manufactured by International Harvester, which no longer makes trucks but is famous for its tractors. In those days, there were no ignition keys – you started the engine with a crank. Before he bought the truck, he had a horse and wagon; his day routinely began at 4:30 a.m. at a nearby stable where he fed his horse and then harnessed him for the daily job of collecting and recycling sacks. The horse was not a pet but, like most horses at the time, a strictly functional creature used to deliver milk and other household goods. Even my sisters never thought of giving our horse a name. In those days, the only horses with names were the ones you bet on at the racetrack.

My father was always long gone before any of the rest of us woke up in the morning and he would routinely come home, exhausted and filthy, as we were getting ready for bed. I seem to remember it taking him most of what was left of his evening just to wash up and he would then go right to bed. My sister Luba recently told me that my father was adamant about never wanting me to do what he did. She added, "He never complained about his job, but that's how I knew how much it must have taken out of him."

I was probably not aware of it as a boy, but I can see now that my parents were very much a team. They were always respectful and supportive of each other. When my father was not at work, he helped my mother around the house, washing the floors, for example, which was not something you saw most fathers doing in those days. He would also get up early to make breakfast for all of us on those rare days when he didn't go to work. I do not remember my parents ever going out to eat or to the movies, but my mother made sure they had a social life with their group of friends, their *landsleit*, fellow immigrants facing challenges similar to their own.

My parents' sense of purpose was hard-won. During their first few years in Montreal, they were in a state of limbo, waiting for their visas to the United States to be approved so they could move to New York. They had already invested in the gas station my grandfather and my uncle were running there. But, as time passed, my parents became increasingly aware that friends and acquaintances who had applied after them and were no more qualified were being granted visas. The longer they waited, the clearer it became that there was a problem. Finally, a customs agent was blunt with my father. "Your family doesn't want you in New York. You are not being sponsored. If you were, you would be there by now."

We never learned all the details but I can guess what was happening. My grandfather was in a bind. My Uncle Boris was already working in the business, which was just not lucrative enough to support an additional family. This rejection, even if there were practical reasons for it, must have hurt my parents, my father in particular, though neither of them ever showed it. Learning what was happening, however, forced my parents to accept that Montreal was their home. If they were to make a future, Montreal was where they were going to make it. Finally, they felt free to settle down and start new lives for themselves and for us.

My older sisters, Luba and Jenny, also taught me about the value of hard work. Both were exceptional role models. Luba, as the first-born, had to grow up quickly. She will tell you that she always felt like a grownup. Even as a girl of seven or eight, she served as a translator, a go-between, and an advisor for her Yiddish-speaking, immigrant parents. "From the time I was born, I was independent," Luba says now, adding:

> I don't remember our mother ever showing me how to do anything. But she didn't have to ask me to do anything either. I would automatically help her. I didn't think about it. I remember, many years later, after I'd become a mother myself, being at a talk about what life was like back then and someone in the audience got up and told the story of how she was the oldest in an immigrant family and about the responsibility that went with that position in the family. I didn't know this woman but I went over to her afterward and thanked her because she had spoken for me. I was glad to hear that someone felt just like I had felt when I was growing up.

Jenny, who was five years younger than Luba, worked hard to conti-nue her education at a time when it was rare for any child of an immigrant, let alone a girl, to attend college. She worked as a bookkeeper during the day and earned her Bachelor of Arts degree from Sir George Williams College (now Concordia University), at-tending classes at night. It took her eight years to graduate, but she did not give up. She persevered and earned her degree.

It was inevitable then that even I – the pampered boy in the family – would have the importance of hard work ingrained in me. How could I not? The family work ethic was everywhere around me. It was the air that I breathed. I do not remember having a lot of friends or playing hockey or baseball like the other kids in the neigh-bourhood. Even as a kid, I was already on what would turn out to be my lifelong career path. It all started simply enough when my cousin, Mendel Severs, who was a year older than me, got a summer job. If he could work, I thought, so could I. I don't remember asking my parents for permission to look for a job – I just got on my bicycle and went to the corner drug store. I met the owner, a pharmacist named Emmanuel Weinrauch, known to everyone as Manny Winrow, a man who would soon become a mentor to me. Manny, with his brother Harry, ran Winrow's Drug Store at 1470 Van Horne Avenue, at the corner of Stuart Avenue. But when I first asked if he needed a messenger boy, I was told he already had one. Still, they took my name. A week later, their messenger boy quit and I was hired. I was ten going on eleven.

Making deliveries was a job, a way to earn a few dollars, but through it I also got to know the Outremont neighbourhood and the people in it in a way I might not have otherwise. I think the job made me aware, early on, of the importance of community. It also gave me a sense, even then, of the value of the local pharmacist. As William Weintraub recounts in *City Unique*, his popular history of Montreal during the 1940s and '50s, some neighbourhood storekeepers "had reputations as psychiatrists, listening to the customers' problems and offering advice."

Of course, I was a kid when I began at Winrow's and often behaved like one. I was lucky to stay out of trouble. Montreal had streetcars then and if you were a kid riding a bicycle and you wanted to get somewhere fast, with minimum effort, you could hang onto the back of a trolley car and let it pull you along, especially if you were headed uphill. I would have one hand on the streetcar, one hand on my bike, and the parcels I was delivering stuffed into my little basket. Obviously, this was not the safest mode of transportation. It certainly was not one my mother would have approved of if she had known what I was up to. But it was fun and adventurous. I remember falling once. I must have turned my wheel the wrong way. It was raining and I ended up on the sidewalk with my bike by the side of the road. A car stopped abruptly to avoid hitting it and I was able to retrieve it. Now, I can recognize what a close call that was.

Another episode stands out from my days at Winrow's Drug Store. I must have been there a few years by then because I was working inside the store. Manny Winrow's niece, Isabel Weinrauch, came in. She was angry about something – I think it was an order she had not yet received – and she accused me of being responsible for the mix-up and of being lazy. She really called me on the carpet. Eventually, I was able to explain to her that I knew nothing about whatever it was she was so upset about. I remember her looking at me, realizing she had made a mistake. She knew better than to accuse me of slacking off. She knew me well enough to know that was the one thing I would never do, the one thing I was frankly incapable of. It was just not in my nature. I still remember her exact words when she eventually acknowledged her mistake. "Morris," she said, "I know that you don't have a lazy bone in your entire body."

I flourished working at Winrow's and for Manny. I quickly graduated from messenger boy to stock clerk – checking merchandise deliveries – and then to serving customers, completing sales and depositing money in the cash register. By the time I was sixteen, I was allowed to be alone in the store – opening and closing the pharmacy and, eventually, dispensing prescriptions. At closing, I would take the day's receipts home in my jacket pocket since Manny was always concerned that someone might break into the store during the night. I was being given more and more responsibility and I loved it.

It was commonplace for pharmacies in those days to have a soda fountain area and one of my more unlikely responsibilities at Winrow's was to work as what was then called a soda jerk. This meant I made sundaes, milk shakes, floats, ice cream sodas, banana splits, you name it, for the customers. One day one of my high school teachers came in and ordered a BLT. The "B," of course, stood for bacon, a food I, as a good Jewish boy, had no previous acquaintance with. Still, I did the best I could. I took out two slices of bread, applied the lettuce and tomato and then slapped two slices of raw bacon into the sandwich, as if it was smoked meat. My teacher took a bite and, thank goodness, started to laugh. Then she gave me the necessary instructions. "You've got to fry it, Morris," she said.

It was my first lesson in non-kosher cooking. This was also, as my son Jonathan is quick to point out, the last time I ever did anything in a kitchen other than eat.

This was just one of the many things I learned at Winrow's. When I got a little older I spent weekends in the pharmacy and when things were quiet I studied the *British Pharmacopeia*, the pharmacist's bible, and memorized all the dosages. It was the kind of thing that would come in handy later in life and gave me a decided advantage on my fellow students when I began attending the University of Montreal to study pharmacy. But if I was a diligent, tireless worker from a young age, I probably should not take too much credit for it. It was second nature. It was part of who I was. It was my inheritance.

I had changed schools three times before I was nine and schoolwork came less naturally to me. I was not a particularly good student in elementary school, although I had improved a little by the time I got to high school, particularly in subjects like math and science, which I enjoyed. Now, I see how I can chalk that up to my natural curiosity, which has also been part of who I am for as long as I can remember and has served me well throughout my career and my life.

English was one of the subjects I struggled with. We spoke Yiddish in our home and I always had difficulty with languages. Looking back on that time, I have no doubt I would have benefited from tutoring. But you have to realize parenting was done very differently in those days. It was not just that tutoring cost extra money my parents did not have – immigrant families did not hover over their children or worry about them in the same way parents do now. Children, especially first-generation children, were expected to succeed on their own.

My parents were concerned, however, with my surroundings. I was only nine but it was not too early for my parents to start thinking ahead to my bar mitzvah, and these thoughts may have given a sense of urgency to their decision to find a new neighbourhood. Simply put, they wanted their son to be closer to a Jewish community. From St. Dominique, we moved to 5220 Clark Street. We also lived, for a brief time, in a mainly Italian neighbourhood, moving north to 7025 St. Urbain Street, in what is now referred to as Little Italy. My parents then went on to buy a triplex at 868 Dollard Avenue in Outremont. The idea was to rent out two of the three flats, which would provide sufficient income so they could live in the third flat rent-free. This was, in the early 1940s, an upgrade in lifestyle for my family and an indication that my father's business was improving. Another attraction of Outremont was its standing as a very strong Jewish enclave. I can guess what must have been on their minds as my bar mitzvah loomed: "We have to give our son a proper Jewish education."

My secular education began with first grade at Fairmount School, on Esplanade and Fairmount, and I attended grade two through five at Edward VII School, on Esplanade near Van Horne. For grades six and seven, I attended Guy Drummond School, on Dollard Boulevard, at the corner of Lajoie, close to our new home in Outremont. It is worth noting that these schools, as well as the high school I attended, were all part of the Montreal Protestant School Board. The educational system in Quebec at the time was organized along religious lines, depending on whether you were Catholic or Protestant and the Catholic School Board refused to accept the new flood of non-Catholic students. It was clearly a decision based on religious preju-

dice and the result was that Jewish children were accepted into the
Protestant school system instead and were educated primarily in English. The Protestant School Board did not act entirely out of altruism
– the more students they attracted, the greater the tax base. These decisions would eventually have profound consequences for Quebec's
political future, especially as the Nationalist movement in Quebec
gained momentum in the 1960s, first with the Quiet Revolution and
later, in the 1970s, with the emergence of the separatist Parti Québe-
cois, with the PQ eventually coming to power in 1976. It is only spec-
ulation on my part, of course, but if French society had been more
open to the Jews when they arrived – if, in other words, Jewish children had been allowed to learn to speak French by attending Catholic
schools – the referendums in 1980 and 1995 might have gone differently. Jacques Parizeau's controversial remarks on the night of the
PQ's 1995 defeat – the separatist side lost, he said, because of "money
and the ethnic vote" – were crude and bigoted but they had a degree
of truth. Ironically, it would be the separatist PQ government that
would change the laws regarding religious school boards. In 1998,
with future Quebec premier Pauline Marois then serving as PQ minister of education, the educational system was restructured, changed
from confessional-based school boards (Catholic-Protestant) to lin-
guistic-based school boards (French-English).

Of course, in the 1940s, when I was attending school, such matters
did not seem important. Montreal, like the rest of the world, was pre-
occupied with the events of the Second World War. Our family gath-
ered every night to sit by the radio and listen to the ten o'clock BBC
news. We were transfixed by reports of Allied victories and defeats
and were also hoping to hear something that might give my parents,
my mother in particular, some glimmer of hope about the fate of her
family and friends in the Ukraine.

Luba had been dating a young man named Gershon Coviensky and
by the time they were married, in 1943, Gershon was already in uni-
form. In grade 10, I joined the Strathcona Air Cadets and became a
bugler in the band. We drilled in the basement of my old elementary
school, the Guy Drummond School Building, and even learned how
to handle rifles. Or, I should say, some of us learned.

One day I was handed a rifle along with a few bullets. Feeling like
a soldier, I aimed at a target and pulled the trigger. But the weapon
was heavy and when it went it off I was jolted backwards. The bullet
ended up hitting a support beam and chipping off a good chunk of

plaster. My target, meanwhile, remained intact. The rifle was immediately taken from me, marking the end of my military career. I have never held a weapon since.

Canadian Jews as a whole made a serious effort. As Joe King writes in *Fabled City*, out of the country's "Jewish population of 167,000 men, women, and children, a high proportion – more than 10% – enlisted in the armed forces ... [some] 16,833 (including 279 women), plus a further 2,000 who felt they shouldn't be identified as Jews if captured. About half of [the enlistees] were from Montreal."

Montreal, in the late 1930s and early 1940s, was not immune to the poison of anti-Semitism that was infecting the rest of the world. I cannot say it was something I experienced directly, but, as I would discover over the years, it was something that was always present.

My father and mother were not what you would call religious Jews. In fact, Luba recalls my father telling her that shortly after the 1917 Russian Revolution, a few years before he, my mother, and my sister left the Ukraine, he had flirted with Communist ideas. It was, however, an unforgiving ideology with which he quickly became disillusioned. What his deepest religious beliefs were I cannot honestly say, but I do know that he started going to synagogue regularly around the time we moved to Outremont so that I would be encouraged to accompany him. It was an example, first and foremost, of how my parents' strategy of education worked: they taught not with words but with deeds.

I remember how action combined with friendship also helped develop new businesses. For instance, there was the time two sons of friends of my parents, members of the Tock family, wanted to start a small business but had neither sufficient funds nor the credit to borrow money from a bank. So they borrowed from their parents' friends, a group that included my parents. With the help of these friends, the two young men went on to build a successful company, one they, in turn, passed on to their children.

Another way Jewish immigrants helped each other was by forming *landsleit* societies. These societies were made up of immigrants who came from the same areas in Eastern Europe. Their regional affiliation helped them to come together and address their social needs as a group. For example, they were able to buy land for burial sites. They were also able to hire a physician on retainer who could look after their medical needs – an early, rudimentary but effective form of health care. The doctor who took care of me when I was born, and whom my parents always considered responsible, along with my mother, for saving me when I was sick, was Dr. Arthur Schlesinger. He remained our family doctor until my parents' deaths.

In the first half of the twentieth century, other institutions were established to address the needs of Montreal's Jewish community. One of the most beneficial of these organizations was the Hebrew Free Loan Association. It started in Montreal in 1911 and had as its prime goal the provision of small, often interest-free, loans to people in need, especially those looking to start a new business. My father benefited from their help when he started his own business. Even though he was running a one-man operation, he still needed funds to get started.

There was also the Yiddish-language newspaper, *Der Keneder Adler*, and the private social club, the Montefiore Club. The Jewish Public Library was built in 1914. A decade later, thirty Jewish physicians, as Joe King writes in *Fabled City*, met to deal with the need for the Jewish community to establish its own hospital. One reason such a hospital was needed was simple: Jewish doctors needed a place to work. When they applied for staff positions at hospitals throughout Montreal, they routinely faced barriers because they were Jewish.

It would take another decade for this dream to be realized but on 8 October 1934 the Jewish General Hospital opened its doors and admitted its first patient. There were ten nurses, King adds, and "they fussed about the patient – not leaving her [side] for a moment, until finally the woman begged the staff to leave her alone ... so that she could sleep."

◆

Like so many men and women of that era, my parents were not demonstrative. They did not say much or openly express their emotions. My father, however, spoke more than my mother and was more sentimental. Luba remembers him pining for his old life in the Ukraine. He would talk about how difficult things were in Montreal and reminisce about picking large cherries from the trees in his small village in the Ukraine as if it were some kind of lost paradise. (He conveniently forgot the ever-present terror of the Cossacks and their periodic visits to that paradise.) But if my father entertained the occasional daydream about returning to the Old Country, my mother would have none of it. She had no intention of going back. Still, she missed her family in the Ukraine and would regularly send them a few dollars to help out. She never stopped hoping that one day her family would join her in Montreal, but her sisters refused to leave because they had boyfriends there. Their future husbands, as it turned out.

Although my parents were not outwardly affectionate toward my sisters and me, there was never any question in our minds that they loved us. They showed their love in the sacrifices they made on our behalf. However, I doubt that they considered what they did for us a sacrifice. In this respect, life was simpler for them: they believed that we, their children, came first. There was no question of that in their minds or in ours. We always had good food to eat and we always had clothes on our backs.

What I remember most vividly about my childhood is that my whole world was contained in a few blocks – Ducharme Avenue to the north, Cote St. Catherine Road to the south, Stuart Avenue to the east, and Rockland Road to the west. I went to school and work weekdays; on Saturday mornings, I went to synagogue. My neighbourhood synagogue, the Adath Israel Congregation, became an important influence in my life during my pre-teen and teen years, though perhaps not in the way that was originally intended. While I went to Hebrew school in the afternoons after regular school, I did not have much success learning Hebrew. I was not especially interested and I was not good at languages. Most of all, though, I was too tired; when I was not in school, I was working at Winrow's.

But from the start I always appreciated the community aspect of the synagogue. In particular, I participated in community singing, joining the congregation in hymns and prayers. Through this activity I learned I had a facility for music as well as a pretty good voice. I loved to sing. I still do. Just ask my wife, Roz, who has been listening to me for over fifty years now and who can be forgiven for being a little tired of hearing me indulge in what remains the favourite part of my personal repertoire – cantorial music. It was at the Adath Israel that I developed a special fondness for this music as well as an appreciation for the role of the cantor in the synagogue. His job, then as now, is to interpret the congregations' prayers in music. I was chosen to be the cantor for the junior congregation and had the opportunity to lead the evening services for our Hebrew School's graduation ceremony in 1944.

The Adath Israel Congregation had met first in 1930 in a rented hall above the Ben Ash Delicatessen on Van Horne, near Wiseman Avenue. The meeting place was a major step forward since many congregations at the time could not afford any kind of communal gathering place. Instead, congregants routinely met in people's homes. But the Adath Israel continued to grow and in 1940 it moved into a brand new building on McEachran Avenue in Outremont, just a short time before my family moved into the neighbourhood.

Born and educated in England, Rabbi Charles Bender became the spiritual leader of the congregation and remained rabbi and then rabbi emeritus until his death in 1993 at the age of ninety-seven, having spent sixty-five years as a rabbi in Montreal. I came to appreciate and enjoy his weekly sermons and a good deal of what he said has stuck with me over a lifetime. I believe Rabbi Bender saw it as his mission to help his entire congregation gain a deeper understanding of the more down-to-earth Jewish values based on the teachings of the Torah. He emphasized modesty, for example, and insisted we not take ourselves too seriously. These were valuable, if not always heeded, messages, especially for rambunctious teenage boys.

"The joy is in the effort rather than the outcome," Rabbi Bender would preach to a congregation that often lived for their chance at upward mobility. You could hardly blame the individual congregants for being ambitious. Mordecai Richler, with his characteristic mix of respect and scorn, liked to describe his classmates at Baron Byng High School as "strivers." And, of course, all of us were striving in our own way. We all wanted something better, something more. It was a dream instilled in us by our parents, our extended families, our friends, our teachers. A dream that started for us with education. But, back then, wanting something better was also Canada's dream, the dream of a young, hopeful country.

These dreams are what made Rabbi Bender's role in the community so essential. He was glad to see that we were high-achievers, but he was also determined to make us into menschen – caring, moral human beings. And so he would say to any of us who were prepared to listen: "Don't build ivory towers. Set goals you are capable of attaining."

I guess I must have been listening. I remember his Saturday sermons to this day. In those sermons, he emphasized the importance of generosity over wealth. One question he liked to ask of the congregation was "Why is a coin round?" Then, after a long, predictable silence, he would reply, "Because it can roll from one person to another." I may not have understood at the time what he was getting at but I have certainly had occasion to reflect on it since. It is an invaluable lesson for anyone who ends up running his or her own business, as I eventually would. He was pointing out to us that even if you have money, you should not be complacent enough to think you will always have it.

I also remember congregants puffing themselves up and saying to him, "You know, Rabbi Bender, my grandfather was a rabbi, too," thinking they could impress him with their spiritual lineage. But his response was always the same: "And, tell me, what are you?"

Even more than the sermons themselves and Rabbi Bender's weekly messages, I remember the impact those sermons had on me. I see it clearly now and I think I must have sensed it then, too, that these sermons were about how to behave – about how a person learns to live a moral, meaningful life. My relationship with Rabbi Bender was a long-lasting one. I eventually became a secretary of the synagogue. I do not know if I would call us close in a conventional sense, but here was a man who knew me for fifty-two years. He watched me grow up. He officiated at our wedding. He saw our children come into this world. He saw something blossoming. It was exactly what he was hoping for; what he was working for. He was always on the lookout for a good-news story, for a reason to qvell, the Yiddish word for taking special pride in others, especially the next generation. I am proud, now, to say that, on occasion, I gave Rabbi Bender reason to do just that.

Spending time at the synagogue as a youngster, I also began to get my first sense, from Rabbi Bender and others, of what is required to be a leader in the community. Joel Sternthal, who was then president of the Adath Israël Congregation, served as a role model for me through his actions much more than his words. He was a true gentleman, who had a dignified, quiet manner, another definition of a mensch. He didn't speak to me directly, but I observed him. His leadership in the synagogue had a positive influence on me just as my parents' actions influenced me, by a kind of osmosis. A successful businessman, he essentially worked two jobs. The synagogue, which he had co-founded, was his second shift. But it was no less important to him. His contributions to the synagogue were extraordinary, so much so a bronze bust of him was placed in the congregation library and remains there to this day.

It helped that the men I met at the synagogue, men in leadership roles in the community, grew to know me a little better. After all, they saw me at the synagogue every Saturday and I had a good voice so they heard me singing. I basically grew up at the Adath Israel and it helped that the older congregants seemed to develop a soft spot for me. They were my mentors, too. They saw that I was active – at the synagogue but also in the neighbourhood, working at Winrow's. I was not just sitting around doing nothing. I was trying to become a more responsible person. They saw potential in me and saw my desire to succeed.

What you do not always realize when you are young is that older people want to help you. If you show interest in them, they will invariably return that interest. At an early age, I had a sense that I wanted to be a leader – a somebody, I guess you could say. I did not want to be just an ordinary person. But I also learned, from men like Rabbi Bender and Joel Sternthal, that I had a responsibility to the community and that part of being successful is to become a contributing member to society. The advice in *Pirkei Avot* (*Ethics of Our Fathers*), a compilation of works written more than 2,000 years ago by famous Jewish philosophers and rabbis like Hillel, became clear to me then and continues to be an influence on the way I live my life: "Do not separate yourself from your community."

3

The Faculty of Pharmacy

Education is not received. It is achieved.
Albert Einstein

The way I would contribute to my community was apparent to me even before I graduated from my high school, Strathcona Academy. I knew I was going to study to be a pharmacist. This was an unusual ambition at the time, especially in Jewish Montreal. In my day the vast majority of the kids, the boys in any case, attending Strathcona were determined to become doctors, lawyers, or, at the very least, accountants. If none of those options worked out, there were always their fathers' thriving shmatte businesses to fall back on.

The advantage I had, of course, was that by the time I was sixteen I was practically an old pro at Winrow's Drug Store. Along with all my other duties, I was already trusted with filling prescriptions. As a consequence, I not only had a clear idea about the career I wanted to pursue, I also had practical knowledge and hands-on experience of that career. For that early advantage, I have Manny Winrow to thank. Roz likes to say that if Manny had been a doctor, dentist, accountant, or, for that matter, a cowboy, I would have probably ended up one too. But I am not so sure about that. Manny was a great mentor to me but it was more complicated than that. Working at the drugstore for as long as I did, and at such a formative stage in my life, gave me the opportunity to be exposed to a profession that few people are acquainted with. There was also something automatic about my relationship with Manny, from the time he hired me as a delivery boy. Part of it may have had to do with the fact that he was a bachelor, something I suspect he regretted. He may have seen in me the son he never had. As for me, I realized early on that you can learn as much from the negative experiences of your mentors as the positive ones. You can learn, in some instances, what not to do and what not to be. I am convinced Manny's *boorching* (Yiddish for griping) about the single life impressed on me the importance of finding a balance between work and family. Similarly, his complaints about the retail pharmacy business likely played a part in my own decision, years later, to get out of the retail business. Thanks to Manny, I think I suspected early on that retail was not for me.

There are all kinds of mentors, all kinds of people you can learn from during the course of your life. Sometimes they don't know the full extent of the impact they have on you; sometimes you don't recognize their impact until much later. Bill Stewart, my high school physics teacher, played such a pivotal role in my life. I was sixteen and in grade 11, my final year at Strathcona, when I started studying for my entrance examination to the University of Montreal's Faculty of Pharmacy. At the time, the University of Montreal was the only university in Montreal where a person could study to be a pharmacist. If I was not accepted there, my only other option was to travel to Laval University in Quebec City. Obviously, this was not my first choice.

It should be added here that McGill University had once had its own College of Pharmacy. But that field of study was affected dramatically when McGill's Dean of Arts, Ira MacKay, decided in 1929 to bar as many Jewish students as possible from attending the university. MacKay, as Allan Levine reports in the *National Post*, 13 September 2013, infamously wrote: "The simple obvious truth is that the Jewish people are of no use to us in this country." His success in imposing quotas for the number of Jewish students admitted to McGill had a particularly adverse effect on the College of Pharmacy, which had a large number of applications from Jewish students. This effect suggests an interesting socio-cultural phenomenon – that at the time gentile students were more likely to enter fields like medicine while Jewish students, facing restrictions in entering medical schools, were filling the void by entering the field of pharmacy. In any case, MacKay's prejudice helped close down McGill's College of Pharmacy for good in 1932. This would have a direct effect on me and others like me, predominantly English-speaking kids, who would have had a much easier time attending McGill. It is also the case, however, that MacKay's bigotry was a blessing in disguise, since the Jewish students he kept out of McGill went to the University of Montreal – a great way to acquire a second language – and were bilingual when they graduated.

The University of Montreal, to its great credit, had no such restrictions, spoken or unspoken, on Jews. In order to enter its Faculty of Pharmacy I was required to pass The College of Pharmacists entrance exam; passing that exam meant I could pursue my chosen career path right away, without first having to obtain a bachelor's degree. That would save me at least four years. So I began, in my final year in high school, to study hard, if a little belatedly, for the entrance exam. About ten days before I was to take it, I acquired some exam papers from previous years to review and recognized that the same question about defining the differences between hydroponics and hydraulics kept showing up on all of the old exams. I was not sure of the answer so after class one day I went to see Mr. Stewart and asked him if he could help me with the question. He took a few minutes to explain the difference to me. Then he asked why I was interested in all this relatively obscure stuff. I told him about my ambition to become a pharmacist and explained that I was studying for the exam to be given in a week by The College of Pharmacists, the licensing board for Quebec pharmacists. I appreciated his help and interest but thought nothing more of it. That Friday night I took a break and went to a movie. When I returned my mother told me that Mr. Stewart had phoned. It was unusual to be called at home by your teacher so I called him back the next morning, curious about what he had to say. I still remember his words. "Morris, you came to me for help yesterday," he said, "and I really didn't provide you with very much information. So if you need more help, I want you to come over to my house and I'll go over anything with you ... anything you need to understand this weekend."

Here, again, in his actions, in his generous offer, was an example of the kind of difference-making behaviour that would stay with me. It was a lesson in the value of extending yourself to others. Even then, I remember being struck by the fact that he would get nothing from making this offer other than the sense of satisfaction that comes from helping someone.

I was grateful to Mr. Stewart at the time, too, though I also had to explain to him that I still was not sure exactly what help I needed. I told him I was just beginning to study. "Mr. Stewart," I confided, "I don't know what I don't know!" Still, his encouragement was enormously meaningful. His interest and concern stimulated me to open my books and start working hard immediately. It was through Mr. Stewart that I learned the difference between those teachers who just went through the motions and those who, like him, gave that extra effort. I know he left a similar impression on many other Strathcona students, and, like all the mentors I encountered as a young man, Mr. Stewart's example would encourage me to make an extra effort to mentor young people throughout my career.

I had only one goal after I graduated from high school and that was to become a pharmacist. Single-mindedness is also a natural-born gift and, in my case, it has had its virtues. If I was not the smartest kid in my class and if I did not always have the family connections or the monetary advantages other kids had, I had the great benefit of always knowing what I wanted to do with my life. I was sixteen and determined to pass my exam, which would then make it possible for me to be accepted into the University of Montreal's Faculty of Pharmacy. That was my ultimate and only goal at that time.

Nothing was going to deter me, not even my own mistakes. For example, there were not a lot of options as to what you could study in high school, but in Grade 10 we were given a choice between taking science or Latin. I jumped at the chance to study science. It was a subject that would always be of particular interest to me. But what I did not know, and what no one had bothered to tell me, was that if I wanted to study to be a pharmacist Latin was a requirement. I learned this when I paid a visit to the College of Pharmacists. As a result, I spent that summer working hard to catch up. This time a tutor was absolutely necessary so I hired one and when I went back to school and took Grade 11 Latin, I was on the same level as my fellow students.

I made another mistake a little later that could not be fixed quite so easily. While I passed the entrance exam and thus became eligible to attend the Faculty of Pharmacy, I registered for my classes one day too late. The first-year classes I needed were already full by the time I realized my mistake. I immediately went to see Alfred Larose, the dean, to appeal to him admit me. I told him I would sit on the stairs during class, if I had to. I just wanted to make up for this oversight on my part. My disappointment at the time demonstrates just how driven, how eager, I was to get started, not just with my education but with my chosen career – in short, with my life. I was lucky then, as I have so often been, even though things seemed to have gone wrong. The dean took one look at me and asked how old I was. I told him I was sixteen and a half, putting a lot of emphasis on that half, but the fact is I must have looked even younger to him. I was, to put it mildly, underweight. I can imagine him thinking, "What this skinny kid needs is a sandwich." But, to his credit, he took me seriously and gave me some good advice. He asked me if I had been accepted to any other universities. I replied that I had not applied to any other pharmacy school because there were no others in the Montreal area. There was one in Quebec City, but living away from home was out of the question. I could not afford that. However, I had been accepted as an undergraduate to McGill and to what was then Loyola College. "Here's what you do: you go to McGill for one year," Dean Larose said, "and after that you'll walk right out of McGill and into pharmacy school here." He could not have been more reassuring. Or right. That is exactly what I did.

And even though I was disappointed at not being able to get started immediately on my education in pharmacy, my year at the famous McGill downtown campus was definitely not wasted. In retrospect, the mistake I had made by not registering at the University of Montreal on time turned out to be one of the best things that ever happened to me. It was one of those occasions, of which there have been many in my life, when it has proven better to be lucky than smart.

McGill broadened my horizons, opening up a world that was much bigger than those four blocks in Outremont where I had been living. If I had been immediately accepted into the Faculty of Pharmacy, it would have been a very focused program. I would never have met the people I met at McGill. For starters, there would have been no time to socialize. Besides, I was not nearly fluent enough in French to socialize in a second language.

Looking back on my younger self, I can see now just how impatient I was. I can also see that it probably would have done me good to continue my McGill education beyond that one year. My life would have been enriched. In fact, I have often passed this advice on to my own children. I have told them to enjoy their years in college and university, years they will never experience again. We are inclined, when we are young, to rush through our education rather than recognizing how enriching it can be.

But the following year, 1949, my own rushed plan continued. I entered the University of Montreal's Faculty of Pharmacy, as the dean of the department had predicted the previous year. In some ways, the

Faculty of Pharmacy was just part of an ongoing apprenticeship that had begun some eight years earlier when I began making deliveries for Winrow's Drug Store. In terms of knowing my stuff, the university coursework was not going to be a problem. I was, at least when it came to my career path, a confident young man.

Still, there were other challenges to overcome. For example, my problem with languages. As I have said, my French was not especially strong. But while the lectures in the Faculty of Pharmacy were in French, the textbooks were in English, which meant that all the students, the vast majority of whom were francophone, were on a somewhat equal footing. Anglophone students were also permitted to take exams in English. Virtually all of the English-speaking students were Jewish and I know that for some of them becoming a pharmacist was a fallback position after they had not been admitted into medical school. In a class of 125 students, there were 9 of us from the same neighbourhood and from similar backgrounds. Women were even more of a minority. I think there were 4 in our class and, if I remember correctly, most, if not all, of them were nuns. In those days in Quebec, it was quite common for the nurses working in the Catholic hospital system to be nuns and the nuns studying to be pharmacists were also expected to work in hospital pharmacies. Quebec society has changed dramatically, of course. The Church no longer has the influence it once did and today women routinely outnumber men in schools of pharmacy. In fact, this is true in all the professions, including medicine.

Among the people I met at the Faculty of Pharmacy was my future partner, Morty Levy. The most successful member of that class was Jean Coutu. Even then, Jean's warmth and ease of conversation shone through. His personality, along with his entrepreneurship, was a key factor in his becoming the most successful pharmacist in the province of Quebec. Later on, when we were both doing philanthropic work, I joked in a speech that at school I beat Jean in marks, but he beat me where it counts – in the marketplace.

Classes were large in those days and students sat in stadium-style lecture halls, seated in alphabetical order, which is how I first encountered a young man named Arthur Goldstein. That proved to be a more auspicious meeting for Arthur than for me. As it turned out, Arthur was less interested in my charms than in the charms of the person I would eventually introduce him to.

As he recalled recently:

The Jewish boys did tend to gravitate to one another and Morris and I became friendly quickly. Anyway, it was September and Morris was an usher at the Adath Israel and he had asked this young woman who attended the same synagogue to take a walk with him on Park Avenue. That was a big deal then. Park Avenue was like a promenade in Montreal. It's where everyone went to be seen, especially on the High Holidays. In fact, every out-of-work rabbi who couldn't make a living opened up his parlor on Rosh Hashanah and Yom Kippur to hold services. There must have been dozens of them in the downtown area where everyone lived. Anyway, I was also walking down Park Avenue and I ran into Morris with this pretty young girl and he introduced us. She and I started to date. Her name was Lorraine and she was my last date. I married her.

I also remember Arthur and I having long talks about what we wanted to do after we graduated from pharmacy school. The future of our profession concerned me even then. I talked to a lot of my fellow students about this subject and about the direction we planned to take once we graduated from university. Arthur also remembers those talks:

Morris and I discussed how we wanted to become ethical pharmacists. I remember we were always discussing what we would like to do. How, for instance, we'd like to run a business. It was our dream. We would just do prescriptions and not sell merchandise or have a soda fountain the way most pharmacies, including Winrow's, did then. But the dream never came to fruition. That's because everyone, once they opened their first pharmacy, had a soda fountain. I had one too when I opened my first pharmacy six months after I graduated. It was not my best financial decision – I ate more than I made.

Arthur also remembers the University of Montreal as a welcoming place. He could not remember encountering any kind of anti-Semitism while he was there. He recounted one incident in which everyone failed a particular test except for the Jewish kids in the class and the teacher, a French Canadian, announced that he was absolutely ashamed of his French Canadian students.

"The class was stunned," Arthur recalled. "The teacher said, 'You have here eight or nine anglophones' – that's the first time I heard the word anglophone used – 'and each of them passed while the entire French Canadian contingent failed.'"

As one of the students who passed that exam, I remember the story a little differently than Arthur. The teacher in question was also working for a multinational pharmaceutical company and he was overseeing a first-year course at the university. He gave a test, which only a few kids passed, just as Arthur said. But the teacher realized he was going to have to give the test again because he could not have the vast majority of his class failing. He explained that the first and the second test would each count for fifty percent. I had received the best grade in the class on the first test and in the second test I finished second or third. That did not bother me but I was curious to know where I had made a mistake because I really thought I had written a perfect paper. I went to ask the teacher about it. To this day, I remember his words. "You people are never satisfied with your marks," he said, defiantly, challengingly. In some ways, the whole world had changed for Jews after the Second World War, but this was still a disturbing reminder that, just a few short years after the horrors of the Holocaust had been revealed, anti-Semitism was still far from being a thing of the past. If it was buried, it was not buried deeply. Sometimes you just had to scratch the surface to hear that denigrating designation – "you people."

Of course, in the 1930s and 1940s this attitude towards Jews was not limited to Quebec society. In their 1982 landmark book *None Is Too Many: Canada and the Jews of Europe, 1933–1948*, noted Canadian historians Irving Abella and Harold Troper reveal how the Canadian government allowed fewer Jewish refugees into the country – some 5,000 – than any other Western country during and immediately after the Nazi era. Worse still, *None Is Too Many* exposes how Frederick Charles Blair, head of immigration at the time, and Mackenzie King, prime minister during the Second World War, conspired to keep Jews out. The title *None Is Too Many* is based on an anecdote in the book about an immigration officer who, when asked how many Jews would be allowed into Canada after the war, bluntly replied, "None is too many."

While it was hardly surprising to find traces of anti-Semitism lingering in institutions in Quebec as well as the rest of Canada in the 1940s and into the 1950s, my friend Arthur Goldstein was right about the University of Montreal being a fundamentally welcoming place. Indeed, it is a place to which I will be forever grateful for the education and the opportunities it provided. My career in pharmaceuticals was launched at Manny Winrow's drugstore, but it would not have gone anywhere without the education I received at the University of Montreal's Faculty of Pharmacy. After graduation, however, I would be the one responsible for transforming my choice of occupations into the kind of career and the kind of life I dreamed it could be.

4

Starting Out: May 1953

We make our own fortunes and we call them fate.
Benjamin Disraeli

In retrospect, I see now that a life can change dramatically in just one month; in my case, it was May 1953. That was when circumstances and possibilities converged, though the stage had been set months, even years earlier. That was when I began to envision a future significantly different from the one being pursued by the majority of my graduating class.

For a start, I already had the feeling that I was not the sort of person who would be fulfilled spending his life working in or, for that matter, owning a pharmacy. This feeling would eventually be borne out after I had owned several pharmacies, but more about that later. What I did know, even while I was still a student, is that I wanted to do something that was more creative than being a glorified shopkeeper. I was not cut out to be a retailer. There was, however, a post–Second World War boom happening in every imaginable field and pharmaceuticals was no exception. The breakthroughs in the research and development of new pharmaceuticals would turn out to be on the cutting edge of everything from health care to social change. R&D (research and development) was the catchphrase for a new era, in much the same way that "innovation" and "start-up" are the current catchwords. In my chosen field, scientific research was leading to a multitude of exciting new drugs and drug treatments. All the energy that had gone into fighting the war was suddenly being redirected to the massive job of reconstructing a world emerging from the darkness of prejudice and mass murder. It felt like a new, enlightened world where possibilities seemed unlimited, where an individual could make a difference. It was a world I knew I wanted to be part of.

Looking back, it is difficult to know what led me to a conclusion like this. After all, I was young and impressionable. It was 1953 and I was only twenty-one when I graduated from the University of Montreal. Nevertheless, I had a head start on my decision to veer away from retail. Having grown up working in Manny Winrow's pharmacy, I already had a taste of what that part of the business was like. And what I had not experienced firsthand for myself, I was hearing about from Manny on a more or less daily basis. His complaints were constant – the long hours and, most of all, how the real profits in the pharmaceutical business were being made by the manufacturers, not the pharmacists.

However, at the same time that I was theorizing about how I would one day become a pharmaceutical manufacturer, I was still tied to the retail pharmacy business. Shortly after I graduated from the University of Montreal, I submitted an article to the Canadian Pharmaceutical Journal outlining my views on how pharmacies were likely to evolve over the next twenty-five years. I no longer have that article nor can I remember exactly what I wrote. But I remember the gist of it and I remember the significance it held for me. I was mapping out the future, as I saw it. A future where there would be clear divisions established between the big superstores, like Walgreens and cvs, which already were taking hold throughout the United States, and the basic dispensing stores that had, as their primary function, filling prescriptions. My article elaborated on the kind of ongoing discussion I had been having throughout my time at university with classmates like Arthur Goldstein and Morty Levy. Looking back, I can see that this article was a kind of personal manifesto. It was my way of mapping out the kind of future I was envisioning for myself. It was me telling myself that I was not, as a recent graduate and a new pharmacist, about to devote all my past effort, all my study, all my work, to selling Chiclets and tobacco. (Yes, pharmacies routinely sold cigarettes in those days and did so happily and profitably. In fact, some still do.) That early article of mine was also an expression of my growing concern that, given the way things were progressing in my chosen profession, there would come a day when pharmacists would be selling everything but snow tires out of their drugstores. A day, incidentally, that has arrived.

So, while I knew in theory what I did not want to do, I still had to figure out what I was going to do. This was a challenge, but one I welcomed wholeheartedly. For as long as I can remember, I have always been in a big hurry to get started, to make my way in the world. Luba had me pegged from the start: I was "a jumpy kid." An ambitious one, too. Manufacturing, in particular, appealed to me, but, obviously, I did not yet have the experience to tackle that aspect of the business. (Incidentally, the manufacturing of drugs was not covered in my university curriculum.) Nor did I have the capital to become a manufacturer. So I thought about what might be the next best thing, namely representing foreign companies, specifically medium-sized U.S. companies that needed representation. I could become their authorized distributor, their "detail man" in Canada.

Of all the terms that could be used to describe what I have done in my long career, detail man is one I still cherish. In the literal sense, to be a detail man meant doing a rather straightforward job. You travelled around the country talking to doctors, providing them with information about your product – as well as samples – and filling them in on the details. At its most basic level, this meant being a salesman. I am not, by nature, a charmer. I am certainly no schmoozer. I was not about to take doctors out for drinks or dinner or spend time with them on a golf course, puffing up their egos. (Frankly, I have never had a great love for golf.) Finesse, as Roz has often pointed out, does not come naturally to me. I am too straightforward, too blunt for that type of thing. But for me the job of detailing implied something more than mere salesmanship. It was connected to being a communicator and an educator. This is the aspect of my job that I have always enjoyed most and have found most fulfilling. It has involved communicating with doctors and the medical community at large, explaining the benefits of a new drug or a new application. Above all, it has meant showing doctors how a particular drug or application would be beneficial to their patients. With the exception of creating new drugs and bringing them to market, I am happiest when I am learning new things and imparting that information to others. There is a Latin proverb I learned long ago that applies here: translated it is "By learning you will teach; by teaching you will learn."

Of course, it is easy to philosophize about all this in retrospect. At the time, I not only had to figure out how I could be an effective salesman but also how I was going to get my business – the distributing and detailing of drugs – off the ground. My first step in that direction was finding a partner. In 1952, I approached Morty Levy, who was of the same mind about the future of pharmacies as I was. The problem was we were both students and both very young; we needed someone with business experience and acumen. So I approached my mentor and long-time boss, Manny Winrow, and asked him if he wanted to go into partnership with Morty and me. For Manny, I think this was just a continuation of the evolving relationship between us that had begun when he hired me as a ten-year-old delivery boy. He agreed to join Morty and me and the Winley-Morris Company was born. The name was arrived at rather simply: Win for Winrow, Ley for Levy, and Morris for yours truly.

The partnership lasted exactly one day, but it provided me with an invaluable lesson in the difference between dreaming up a business and actually running one – between theory, the kind of things I was studying in school and writing papers about, and practice, also known as the art of functioning in the real world. In the real world, I discovered that human behaviour has a way of complicating matters. In this case, Morty and I, as working partners in Winley-Morris, felt we should be paid for our time while Manny, essentially a silent partner, felt that since he was not taking a salary, we should not receive one either. This was entirely unrealistic since Morty and I were going to be working full-time at Winley-Morris, while Manny was not. We learned quickly that this disagreement was not going to be resolved. As a result, Manny bowed out and Morty and I bought his shares. We both invested $250 in Winley-Morris.

Our new company was registered in 1952 – we decided to keep the name Winley-Morris; it had a ring to it – while we were still university students. We were also looking for opportunities to make licensing agreements with companies developing patented pharmaceuticals. A week before Morty and I graduated, in May 1953, Winley-Morris got its first big break when we obtained the right to be the Canadian distributor for Stiefel Laboratories, which would, in the years to come, become one of the largest manufacturers of dermatological products in the world. By the twenty-first century, Stiefel had sales of close to one billion dollars, but when we began our relationship with them the company had just two products on the market: Oilatum Soap and Acne-Aid Soap.

At the time I first became involved with Stiefel Laboratories, the company was financed by a venture capital group out of New York City, which had the controlling interest. Around 1958, Stiefel developed an acne scrub called Brasivol. In 1960, the product came to the attention of the Vicks company, who were interested in obtaining the rights to this product. The New York financiers were, as a result, interested in selling Stiefel to Vicks. But the Stiefel brothers wanted to build a business for themselves and went to great lengths to secure the funds to buy out their New York investors. They asked me if I would invest in their company. I invested $20,000 for approximately 5 percent of the company and became a board member. I kept most of those shares until the Stiefel company was sold by Charles Stiefel, Werner Stiefel's son, to Glaxo Smith Kline in 2009. I had held the shares almost fifty years before selling. Part of the proceeds I received was invested in the Rosalind and Morris Goodman Family Foundation, a foundation we created in 2005 mainly to fund our commitments to various charities. One of the lessons I learned early in life was to invest in companies with strong leaders such as the Stiefels, who had both the vision and the passion to build for the future. Incidentally, Warren Buffett learned the same lesson. He made this philosophy the cornerstone of his investment policy.

I still cherish a photograph from that first meeting with the Stiefels. It was taken at Montreal's Ruby Foo's Restaurant, a Chinese restaurant located on Décarie Boulevard and particularly popular with Jewish Montrealers, and captures the moment our crucial deal with Stiefel Laboratories was inked. At the table are Morty Levy, his wife, Pearl, Werner Stiefel, the great-grandson of the company's founder, John David Stiefel, and me. What strikes me is how young I look, how wet behind the ears. I can only marvel now at how much drive and confidence both Morty and I had.

Those were heady days. You could say I was having my cake and eating it too. I was earning $125 a week working mornings, nights, and weekends at Manny's pharmacy – a pretty good salary back then for a young single man – and in the afternoons I was visiting dermatologists, detailing them on behalf of Winley-Morris's brand new client, Stiefel Laboratories. I was also living at home with my parents and not paying for food, board, clothes, or anything else, as a matter of fact. As a result, everything I saved I invested in Winley-Morris.

The obvious question is when did I sleep? Well, I didn't. Who wanted to anyway?

Adding to my lack of sleep was the fact that by the end of Winley-Morris's first month the company had become a one-man operation, that one man being me. Right after graduation, Morty's first child, Stephen, was born. At the same time, Morty received an offer to become a fifty percent partner in a drugstore being built on Sherbrooke Street East, east of Pie IX, not far from where Montreal's Olympic Stadium is today. This was a big opportunity for Morty since the drugstore would be an integral part of the second shopping centre built in Montreal. (The first built by the Cummings family, was the Norgate Shopping Centre, located in Ville St. Laurent.)

Once again, the human variable altered our supposedly perfect start-up business model. Simply put, Morty had a wife and a baby to support and he needed money. And earning money was the one thing we had yet to do at our burgeoning new company. Morty told me he could not afford to work for nothing while we were building our business and he had to do what he thought was best for his family. I was disappointed but I could hardly argue with him. At the same time, he could hardly argue with the fact that I needed a working partner, not a silent one. He took the partnership in the new drugstore and I gave him back his $250 investment in Winley-Morris. Our partnership was officially dissolved. But, like the majority of the business relationships I have entered into that have not worked out for one reason or another, Morty and I stayed on good terms. In fact, when I finally did become a part owner of a retail pharmacy a year later, it was on Morty's recommendation. This stands, I believe, as a testament to the people we both are and to our friendship. It was also an early indication of how I knew I wanted to conduct my business dealings. I wanted to be able to do what was best for me, of course, but at the same time I wanted to be sure to consider the other person's situation as well.

Six months after Morty left Winley-Morris, I introduced a product called Tucks to the Canadian market. I had been introduced to Tucks as a result of attending my first meeting of the American Academy of Dermatology in Chicago. I was there because of my affiliation with Stiefel, but I was also looking for new business opportunities. I did not have far to look – opposite the Stiefel display was an exhibit by a company called Fuller Pharmaceuticals. I met their president, John Fansler, and we chatted. He explained to me how his father, a proctologist, would prescribe witch hazel soaked in cotton balls to treat painful hemorrhoids. The junior Fansler had taken the treatment a step further – developing his own version, using a non-woven pad saturated with a witch-hazel solution. He called this new product Tucks Medicated Pads. I found the story fascinating and asked Fansler if Winley-Morris could represent him in Canada.

"And why you?" I remember him asking. "Why should I look to you as a distributor? After all, I have other offers from more established distributors."

This was a good question for which I, fortunately, had a good answer. "Well, yes," I told him, "those other distributors are well-established and, frankly, Mr. Fansler, they don't need your product. But I do. I need it so I'll work harder." My approach, characteristically straightforward, worked.

"A good reason," Fansler conceded. "I'll give you the rights to Tucks."

Although I was new to making deals, this one also provided a valuable lesson in how I wanted to do business. With any deal, small or large, the paperwork is really just legal mumbo-jumbo. In my experience, a good business deal is always based on one thing and one thing alone – the good will of the people involved.

Winley-Morris signed a distribution agreement with Fuller Pharmaceuticals and began importing and selling Tucks. Almost a decade later, though, it became clear that it was too costly to import the product, in particular because of the mandatory import duty that was attached to drugs from the United States in those days. (This was long before the free trade agreement between the two countries.) So, in a preview of the future business practice of Winley-Morris, I signed a royalty agreement with Fuller and became a manufacturer.

I already had some experience of manufacturing a product on my own from a few years earlier, except at that time the laboratory was in my mother's kitchen, where I mixed up a treatment for acne. I took cosmetic cases and filled them with foundation cream, which had sulphur as its active ingredient. I dubbed it the Acne Pack.

In the case of Tucks, a new employee, George Montgomery, who still works for me at Pharmascience more than fifty years after we first met, helped me mix the formula in the basement of a barbershop next to the drugstore we rented at 6579 Somerled Avenue in the west end Montreal region of NDG. George's wife, Micheline, was also present in our little manufacturing venture, as was Ted Wise, who would, some twenty-five years later, be my partner in the startup of Pharmascience. As for Tucks, it is still manufactured and sold worldwide by Pfizer and remains an effective treatment for hemorrhoids.

George Montgomery is a jack-of-all-trades. He did everything in those days and the variety of his tasks – packaging pills, mixing acne cream, working in my pharmacies – demonstrated that Winley-Morris was a growing concern. However, it was growing slowly. George recently recalled how small the operation truly was in those early days:

> There were probably six of us altogether. That includes my mother as a secretary, Victor Forget, Ted Wise, Doris Jennings, who was Morris's secretary, and Morris. It was the early 1960s and I remember what Morris said to me once about how he only wanted one thing for the business. He wanted it to get bigger.

A major step in that direction for Winley-Morris came in 1953 as a result of a simple act of good will. I was doing my usual morning shift at Manny Winrow's drugstore at the time when I received a call from Dr. Jack Rubin, a pulmonologist at the Royal Edward, a hospital located on St. Urbain Street, below Pine Avenue. Dr. Rubin wanted to know if I could get him a bottle of Parasal-INH, a combination drug used in the treatment of tuberculosis, from the United States. I checked with Manny about placing the order. No doubt Manny thought ordering a single bottle of medication was not worth our time or trouble and he told me to forget about it. But I didn't. In December of 1953 I was about to travel to the U.S., first to Chicago and the American Academy of Dermatology Conference, and then to New York for the wedding of my cousin Sima Chercass. I called Dr. Rubin before I left and reminded him of his earlier request for Parasal-INH. He asked if I could bring back two bottles from New York for him. At the time, I didn't think of this as anything more than a favour for a local doctor. But it was a gesture that would end up paying significant dividends for me and for Winley-Morris.

Once I arrived in New York, I made my way to the offices of Panray Corporation, the manufacturer of Parasal-INH. The company was located on 340 Canal Street in a building that looked like it was about to fall down any minute. I met with Myron Pantzer, the president of the company, who wanted to know who had sent me. I gave him my business card and explained that I was a pharmacist in Montreal and was just doing a favour for a local doctor. He noticed that my card said I represented Stiefel Laboratories and he asked me how things were going. I told him I was getting by, selling a few bars of soap here and there. But our small talk then ended abruptly; Pantzer's next question was a stunner.

"How would you like to represent Panray and Parasal-INH in Canada?" he asked out of the blue.

Of course, I immediately realized what kind of opportunity this was – the chance to distribute an effective treatment for tuberculosis in Canada. But I was also hesitant. "Mr. Pantzer," I said, "I know nothing about such drugs."

"Don't worry," he said, "we'll teach you."

As usual, I was eager to learn. And what I learned, most importantly, was that while TB patients in Canada had been taking forty-four tablets a day of other, earlier, medications, they were only required to take seventeen tablets of Parasal-INH. There were also fewer side effects – for instance, fewer gastric problems – connected with the new drug combination I was about to introduce to the Canadian market.

So Winley-Morris began distributing Parasal-INH. A tip-off as to how successful it would turn out to be came when I received my first order – which came in before I had even officially started promoting the drug. The order was from Prince Edward Island and was for ten bottles. We sold them for $12.50 each so that first sale was for $125. In those days, for me, that was a world of money. Remember, I was accustomed to selling prescriptions for 50 or 90 cents or $1.50, tops. Now, here I was receiving an order for one hundred times that. My profit on that order was $75. My first thought was "Oh boy, this is going to be a good business!"

I did not know the half of it. At the end of the day, you succeed in the pharmaceutical business when you are able to provide doctors with a better treatment than what they are already using and that is what Winley-Morris started out doing. Ultimately, the Ontario and Quebec Ministries of Health became our biggest customers for Parasal-INH – purchasing millions and millions of tablets. Winley-Morris eventually became the number one supplier of anti-TB agents in Canada. We also started manufacturing Parasal products in Canada, paying a royalty to Panray, in order to avoid the import duties. This arrangement was much like the one Winley-Morris had with Tucks, just on a much larger scale.

In 1954, when Winley-Morris first started distributing Parasal-INH, TB was still a terrifyingly contagious, sometimes lethal disease. (It remains so in much of the developing world.) Back then, TB patients were isolated, treated in sanatoriums rather than in their homes. That meant I had to go where the patients and the doctors treating them were. A few years later, I would hire trusted salesmen like Victor Forget and Ted Wise to do the bulk of the traveling. In the early days, however, I criss-crossed the country numerous times as the detail man for Parasal-INH. I flew into towns and small cities everywhere and then rented a car in order to drive well outside the city limits to where the sanatoriums were located. It was, among other things, an education in this country's unique and inspiring geography. In those days, I was making my flights in a DC-3, which meant I was flying at 5,000 and 10,000 feet above the ground, not 30,000 feet like today. I would routinely sit by the window and gaze out at the Great Lakes, the Prairies, the Rocky Mountains, and marvel at the country's vastness and beauty from coast to coast. And I remember saying to myself: "All I have to do is want this. That's all I have to do to succeed. It's all there, open to me. All of it! What's more, everyone is free to partake. What a great, great country this is!"

Yes, I was young and tireless and enthusiastic. I had everything I wanted. Most of all, I had the chance to do something that mattered in people's lives and in the life of this growing country. Oh, how I appreciated Canada! And how I still do!

5

New Ventures

Love does not consist of gazing at each other, but in looking outward together in the same direction.

Antoine de Saint-Éxupery

I have no doubt Roz's memory of how we first met is more vivid than mine. So I will let her tell the story. Here it is, then, in Roz's own words, the more or less official version:

> I was going out with someone who was singing in the choir at the Shaar Hashomayim Congregation and afterward there was a little Kiddush, coffee and cake, that kind of thing. It was a regular Friday night gathering aimed at young people. Anyway, I found myself sitting across from this fellow who was a bit older, and he asked my name, then he asked me where I grew up. He was kind of impertinent, you could say, but obviously I didn't mind chatting with him. So I told him that I grew up in Outremont, on Wiseman Avenue. And he said, "770 Wiseman?" That really freaked me out. I remember thinking to myself: how could he possibly know that? I hadn't thought about that address in years. "I probably delivered your diapers," he continued. I don't know if I was blushing. I do know that I was intrigued. Then he told me all about working at Winrow's Drug Store and doing deliveries for our family pharmacist, Manny Winrow. At which point I said, "I'm guessing my mother gave you a pretty good tip. I'm betting that's how you remember the address." And Morris just smiled. It was a nice smile.
>
> I was attending McGill at the time and I was very studious and conscientious. I made it a point to never go out during exam

period, so when he called me after that first meeting I told him I definitely couldn't see him. I told him that was my rule. But then he called back and we did go out. I guess I broke my own rule. Morris made a very good first impression. I'd never been out with anyone who was more than two or three years older than me, but he was ten years older. He was so worldly. I had the feeling he'd been everywhere and I guess he had, certainly compared to me. He had been across Canada – from Newfoundland to British Columbia. He'd been to Italy, even Israel. He was so intelligent, that was evident right away. And, yes, I also thought he was cute and a great dancer. That was of major importance at the time – being able to dance. He also loved to laugh and sing and I remember he had a lovely white Chevy convertible. Put all those things together, you could say he wasn't a bad catch.

As I said, Roz has a far better memory for this sort of detail than I. But I cannot say I mind hearing her version of things again, even if I am the one, now, who is blushing. I do remember that I proposed almost right away. We could not have been seeing each other for more than a few months. I also remember Roz's father, Joseph Druker, was not especially pleased that his daughter, his only child, was seeing me. He was nervous about her not finishing her education at McGill so he managed to postpone our wedding plans. We became engaged on 15 Februrary 1961 and we were married at the end of Roz's second year at McGill on 8 June 1961. I guess you could say her father and I ended up going 50-50 on paying for Roz's education.

By Roz's fourth and final year we were about to start a family. In fact, our oldest daughter, Deborah Lynn (Debbie), born on 3 November 1962, had a front row seat on her mom's lap when Roz graduated from McGill in May 1963. I like to think this makes Debbie an honorary McGill alumnus.

But, again, I will let Roz describe what the experience of being newly wed and newly pregnant was like:

I was only eighteen when Morris and I became engaged. Until then, I really never thought about getting married. I never even knew anyone, not one of my friends anyway, who was married. I was the first one of my group to take the big step. I also remember that in those days it was a very big deal to be pregnant and going to school. It was simply unheard of. Everyone was scared

of me. To be honest, I was scared of myself. I was walking the
halls of McGill, going to classes, wearing all kinds of borrowed
maternity clothes from my friend Jessica Miller. I was feeling,
well, very out of place, but I was also happy. Really happy.
Morris made things easier for me by always encouraging me to
continue my education. That was unusual for a man to do at that
time. In fact, I know it was very important to him that I continue
my education. I do believe that if I had wanted to go further in
my education, he would also have supported me completely,
whole-heartedly.

   Morris has always been a man who knows what he wants and
when it came to getting married, he knew it was the right time.
I was much more impulsive about the decision than Morris. I'm
the kind of person who just jumps in and then sees the rocks.
That's basically what I did when I married Morris. Now, I think
it was just luck that it all worked out. It had to be. I was so
young. But Morris seemed to know exactly what he was doing
and what he wanted. He was much more methodical about getting married, much more analytical about it than I ever was.

But I wonder now: was I? All those years before I met Roz, I had
been keeping my head down, buried in my work. My only priority
was Winley-Morris. I ate, slept, and dreamt my business. I focused
all my time and energy on making it a success. I had no interest in a
long-term relationship until I met Roz. I went out on dates with other
girls, of course, but it was never serious. But Roz was undeniably
special. Falling in love with her was the most natural thing in the
world.

   To be honest, I was probably also multi-tasking before anyone had
ever heard of such a term. Back then, it was just called staying busy.
In any case, I was branching out. As I mentioned in the last chapter,
I opened a pharmacy a year after I graduated from the University of
Montreal on the advice of my old Winley-Morris partner, Morty Levy.
Morty telephoned one day to say Montreal's Reitman family, who
were prominent in the women's wear retail business and in real estate,
were about to begin construction on a number of buildings on
Somerled Avenue and they were looking for someone to open a retail
drug store. It seemed like a good opportunity, so I took Morty's ad-
vice and became partners in this new venture with my old boss,
Manny Winrow, and Allan Schmeltzer, another Strathcona high

school classmate. Winrow's Drugstore on Somerled Avenue in NDG opened in May 1954 and a decade or so later we brought in another partner, Michel Bougie. As a student, Michel worked at one of the drugstores in the Ellendale Medical Building on Côte-des-Neiges Road that Manny, Allan, and I owned. After Michel graduated and became a full-fledged pharmacist, he also worked in the store I co-owned with Allan in the Rosemere Shopping Centre, a centre owned by Ivanhoe, a subsidiary of the Steinberg's retail food chain. I probably see Michel more now than when he worked for me or later with me as a partner and he could tell you how infrequently I visited the pharmacies I co-owned in those days. Michel and I were talking about this recently and he recalled the time renovations were being done in the Rosemere pharmacy and I came in to help out for the weekend. As Michel said:

Morris rolled up his sleeves and stayed the whole weekend, re-stocking the shelves. I was really struck by that – by how he didn't mind getting his hands dirty. He just didn't want to be in retail on a permanent basis. That was also clear. That was the message I always got.

Michel could not have been more right. To be honest, I do not even remember Michel working in Rosemere, which is probably another indication of my lack of genuine interest in the retail business. Eventually, Allan and Michel, by mutual agreement, bought out my share of the store on Somerled since I was, as Michel correctly pointed out, never around. A business relationship, I have learned, is not very different from any other relationship. You have to give it your full attention, make time for it. Fortunately, Michel, Allan, and I have remained good friends. In fact, Allan and Michel remain my personal pharmacists and among Pharmascience's best customers.

Reminiscing, Michel was also kind enough to add, "I've always felt that if I come to an agreement with Morris, a handshake will do and he will honour that handshake way, way into the future."

As for my experience in retail pharmacy, I suppose it should have taught me that that side of the business was simply not for me. But, about some things, I can be a slow learner. To be honest, I suppose there was a part of me that wanted to see my name in lights. That has always been my personal joke, but there is something appealing about having your name on the front of the store for the public to see. I also saw the retail business as a good investment in those days. After all, I was newly married and starting a family. So I continued to try other retail ventures throughout the 1960s. It was during that period that I opened a pharmacy in the new medical building on Côte des Neiges in partnership with Allan and Manny. Unfortunately, these new ventures invariably ended up causing more problems than they were worth. At the Rosemere store, for instance, Allan and I took on another pharmacist as a partner, a partner who then proved to be untrustworthy and badly mismanaged the business. The final straw was learning that he was drinking while filling out prescriptions. Allan and I had no choice but to sell the store. We ended up absorbing the full loss but we repaid all our creditors in full. In retrospect, I can see that I should never have gone into retail pharmacy. I never made any money owning drug stores. (More often than not, I lost money.) One problem was that I chose partners who were competently trained pharmacists but were not trained in business practices. When I went to pharmacy school no one was educated in how to run a retail business and very few pharmacists took the trouble to learn. In those days, pharmacists were simply not aware of financial controls. They were trained professionals, running their drugstores as if they were running Mom-and-Pop candy stores.

In Quebec, the retail pharmacy changed dramatically, reinventing itself, when pharmacists like Morrie Neiss, with his Cumberland Drugs chain, and Jean Coutu, my fellow University of Montreal alumni, class of 1953, brought the retail business into the twenty-first century. Eventually Jean Coutu bought out Cumberland and became the true king of retail pharmacy in Quebec.

As for me, it only took about a quarter of a century to realize retail was not for me. As I said, I can be a slow learner. It really came down to my lack of genuine passion for the world of retail. I was not prepared to pay as much attention to the daily routine as I should have. As Roz would learn, sometimes to her chagrin, routines are not my strong suit. I get bored with them quickly. I thrive, instead, on problem-solving; in particular, on the next big challenge. And, for me, that would always be Winley-Morris. Over the next few years, Winley-Morris grew – steadily but slowly. Meanwhile, I was pushing thirty, which may explain why, when I finally did lift my head up to look around. I started to realize that my life was not full so much as it was busy. There was also Manny Winrow's example – one I had noticed when I was just a kid, but which had stayed with me – to remind me of what my future would be like if I did not make some significant changes in the way I was living my life. Manny, a lifelong bachelor, had often warned me, sometimes with his words, sometimes with his actions, not to do what he had done. "Get yourself married, have a family," he said, in the occasional conversations we had about personal matters. These conversations were, I can see now, very close to father-son talks. And then, of course, good luck and good timing interceded. I met Roz.

I would be remiss if I did not mention the impact my father's death had on me. This happened just a few months before I met Roz. In fact, I had gone to synagogue to say Kaddish for my father on the evening I was to meet my future wife.

My father's death in 1959 at the age of sixty-five was a tremendous shock, all the more so because I was the only one with him in our house in Outremont when he collapsed. I remember he called my name, but by the time I got to him, he was gone. He had had a massive heart attack.

This was not my first intimate experience with death – when I was eighteen, my best friend, Nathan Berkow, was hit by a car and killed, a terrible tragedy – but the loss of a father is an inevitable milestone. My father's death jolted me into the realization that it was time to start looking for more balance in my own life. I was already a responsible young man – I had been working since I was ten. But after my father's death my perspective changed. And so did my responsibilities. I was suddenly the head of the family and I was also the keeper of our family's memory. It was the role I was born to fulfill, after all. I was the *Kaddishele*. A Jewish family like mine, while not religious in the strict sense of the word, can nevertheless be deeply traditional. Saying the Kaddish for the proscribed eleven months after my father's death was my way of honouring that tradition and honouring him. The Kaddish is a ritual designed to make you think – "Out of tears, thoughts," the writer Leon Wieseltier said in his memoir, *Kaddish*, about his experience praying for his late father – and that is just what it does. You have time to think about what matters and about how your life can matter. I was going to synagogue and saying the memorial prayer twice daily. The truth is the Kaddish prayers serve as excellent group therapy for the bereaved. I can vouch for that.

When Roz and I married in June 1961, Rabbi Bender, who had known me since I was a boy, officiated. For our honeymoon, Roz and I crossed the Atlantic Ocean on the Empress of Britain. I have always mixed business with pleasure and that trip was no exception. Fortunately, Roz got used to this practice early in our marriage and she has never complained about it. On vacation, she will typically get a guidebook and spend the day sightseeing, visiting museums, shopping, but we always meet up again for dinner. Those dinners with Roz remain, to this day, a reminder of how lonely my bachelor days were and how full my married days have been.

Our five-week honeymoon began in Milan, Italy, with an opportunity to make contacts there. We went on to Israel and to a meeting with the Assia Chemical and Pharmaceutical Company, later renamed Teva Pharmaceuticals. This meeting in particular marked the beginning of a productive, lifelong association with Teva and with Israel. Roz and I also took time to tour the country in an old rented army jeep, picking up hitchhikers, having coffee in the homes of Druze Arabs. It was an eye-opening experience, an education – at times sobering, at times exhilarating.

One day we went to Caesarea, a historically renowned port in Roman times, to see the ruins. While we were there we noticed a black-bearded man perched on a tractor, clearing a large piece of land. Roz got out of the jeep to see what was happening and her high heels immediately sank into the sand. It took some doing to extricate her from this sacred sinkhole. We later learned that we had been inadvertent witnesses to history. We had been at the site of the archaeological dig that would eventually uncover the Caesarea Roman amphitheatre built by King Herod, who reigned a few decades before the birth of Jesus. It was a fascinating and unexpected glimpse into the unveiling of a chapter of ancient Jewish history.

We also got a glimpse of modern Jewish history – the 1961 trial of Adolf Eichmann, the Nazi war criminal charged with arranging the mass deportation of European Jews to death camps in Eastern Europe. In 1946, a year after the Second World War ended, Eichmann, who was in American custody, though under an assumed name, escaped. He lived in a variety of places, but ended up in Argentina in 1950 and lived there until 1960, when he was captured during a daring mission by Israeli Mossad agents and returned to Jerusalem to stand trial for crimes against humanity. His trial was open to the public, which is how Roz and I ended up attending. His capture and trial were major international news stories and attending the trial felt like participating in both a dark and ultimately redemptive moment in history. Eichmann's trial also helped bring much needed attention to the crime of the Holocaust, which was tragically overlooked in the years immediately following the war. Eichmann was found guilty and hanged on 31 May 1962, the only person in Israeli history to be given the death penalty by a civilian court.

What we witnessed in Israel demonstrated how so much of the past is part of the present in Israel, a country for which I immediately felt a special emotional bond.

Once Roz and I returned to Montreal, we quickly settled into domestic life. Our first home was a two-bedroom apartment at 3655 Ridgewood Avenue in Montreal's Côte-des-Neiges district, where Roz immediately enjoyed cooking and entertaining. Her enthusiasm, which was considerable, made for some interesting moments since she had never really cooked before and her plans occasionally backfired. For instance, while preparing one of our first meals in our new home, Roz nearly burned down the kitchen, staining our newly wallpapered walls. From the beginning, Roz was a conscientious housekeeper, sometimes too conscientious. There was the time, for example, when my wedding band ended up in the incinerator with the rest of the garbage. It was gone for good.

Roz will tell you that I do not need external things to be happy. The truth is I seldom take much note of my surroundings. She admits to finding it amazing how little space I take up. I admit I have not always been aware of my wife's impeccable taste – as evidence of this my son Jonathan likes to remind me that the master bedroom in my house is pink and I sleep in a canopy bed. Still, I have always been enormously grateful for the ways in which Roz has made the places we have lived both homey and aesthetically pleasing.

My youngest daughter, Shawna, is a long-time observer of her parents and she will tell you that what Roz and I have is rare. It is very much a partnership. Here's how Shawna sees it:

My mom is queen of the house. She creates the social life. She keeps the traditions. She is always present in the house. I can't remember a time when she wasn't. My father is the provider. He loves our house in Hampstead, how it's put together, for instance, but he has no clue how it got that way. I sometimes think he could live in a box and be happy. He is the most low maintenance person you will ever meet. He could also eat a can of corn for lunch every day … and, not only that, he would love it. Still, he also has an appreciation for beauty. My mother taught him that. She allowed him to appreciate things he never would have appreciated otherwise: colour, intimacy, friendships.

The partnership between Roz and me was not only part of our home life but also of business, especially during the early days of Winley-Morris. I have not always been good at making my employees feel appreciated and when I neglected to do that, Roz was on hand to do the job for me. Here is how she remembers her role:

> When we were first married, I was totally in the loop. I really tried to be nice to all the employees. I was afraid they would all quit on us. I'd say to them, "Do you know Morris just thinks you are fabulous?" My job was keeping everybody happy.
>
> While it was true that he did feel that way about his employees, Morris is a man of few words and even fewer compliments. You have to understand, with Morris, he just expected people to do their jobs, the same way he did. He doesn't need that kind of approval, so he doesn't always realize that other people need to feel valued.

Thinking back, now, on the early years of my marriage, what I remember most is how much fun they were. It was the early 1960s, I had a convertible, and I loved nothing more than piling my kids, in their pajamas, and all the neighbours' children too, into the back seat and driving to St. Aubain and Elmridge Dairy for ice cream. Of course, it was easy to fit all the kids in the car in those days because there were no seat belts to get in the way.

By 1964, we had moved to a bigger home at 4175 Jean-Brillant, also in the Côte-des-Neiges area. Our son David was born there on 2 July 1964; Jonathan followed on 9 August 1967. In 1969, we bought the house that we still live in at 111 Finchley Road in Hampstead and that is where our youngest daughter, Shawna, was born on 15 May 1971.

We were a growing, happy family, enjoying our lives. I was still working hard and, while I probably did not see it this way at the time, I realize now that I had begun to merge my philosophy in business with my philosophy of raising a family. The underlying theme in our home was that everyone tried their best at whatever they endeavoured to do. And everyone's contribution mattered.

I have no doubt some people describe me as a workaholic. But I have to confess – I do not know what the word means. It simply did not exist when I was growing up. My parents certainly would never have considered working too hard or working too much as something to be concerned about. In fact, when I had my own children it was natural for me to instil in them the same positive feelings about hard work that had been instilled in me. None of my children, I am proud to say, have any regrets about the way they were raised. My daughter Debbie, my eldest, speaks for her brothers and sister when she recounts what it was like to be the child of a so-called workaholic.

We always knew my father loved to work. We just knew it was a passion for him. It was never a burden. In fact, it was a hobby for him, too. I remember a treat for me was going with him on Saturday afternoons to the office at Winley-Morris. This was when I was five or six. You can't do this kind of thing anymore of course, but I remember he'd put us, me and my brother David, on the assembly line and we'd stuff cotton into pill bottles. Or we'd put the bottles in the boxes. Sometimes we'd just sit in the secretary's office and use the Xerox machine or punch holes. That was the best. We loved it. I loved it. I'm certain it impacted the way we all are. For my brothers and sister and me, going to work was and still is a fun thing to do. We never resented it when he was at work. It was all part of the way we lived our lives. I remember he'd come home from the office at seven and we kids had already eaten at five – we were ravenous. But I would sit with him while he ate his dinner. The thing that has to be pointed out about my father is that, yes, he may have been a workaholic, but he still always made sure his kids didn't feel the least bit neglected. He balanced family and business so well.

My daughter Shawna, our youngest, almost nine years younger than Debbie, has similar memories. She would come into the office on Sundays with Jonathan, who is closer to her in age. Like Debbie, she also remembers sitting with me when I came home late from work:

That was my time with my father. I'd give him dinner if my mother was out, and I'd sit with him and do my homework. We would catch up. Yes, sure, he was a workaholic. But he didn't and still doesn't see this as a negative. Never had a grumpy day going to work that I remember. There was never a day he didn't want to go into the office. That's remarkable. Even on vacation we'd end up scouring the local pharmacies, checking out the competition, wherever we were.

If I succeeded in instilling in my children pride as well as pleasure in the work they do, I also tried to instil in them the importance of finding meaning in that work. It was never about making money, not primarily. Again, Shawna can attest to that:

> We never talked about money in our house. I don't remember my father having a wallet. Money was just there loose on my father's nighttable. There was trust. He would just say to us, "Take what you need." The thought of abusing this trust never entered our minds. This was true for all of us. And that was unusual for kids. But that was my father's attitude toward money. You used it when you needed it. It's to be respected, but it's only there to serve a purpose. It certainly doesn't drive my father, not then, not now. What drives him? The desire to build something – the thrill of making something happen, something that is going to matter, that's what drives my father.

Roz is owed most of the credit for the fact that I have managed to maintain my commitment to both family and work. But, more than that, she has been an integral part of the growth of all three of my ventures into the pharmaceutical business. She has been a partner, in the truest sense of the word, filling the gaps that have existed in my own social skills as a businessman. Her passion for making friends, her effusiveness in the company of people, as well as her talent for entertaining and networking have been crucial to my success in business. Roz and I have also travelled the world together and her enthusiasm for new places and new people has been invaluable, as has her steadfast and creative counsel. There is no doubt in my mind that of all the decisions I have had to make in my life the best one, as well as the easiest one, was asking Roz to marry me.

6

Building a Business

The man who has confidence in himself gains the confidence of others.
Hasidic saying

Just as my fellow pharmacy students and I were woefully unprepared by our university education to take on the demands of a retail business, I also faced unexpected challenges in building Winley-Morris into a successful company. The first lesson I had to learn the hard way – I could not do everything myself. I had to learn how to delegate responsibility and, perhaps more important, that such delegating was necessary.

The notion of self-reliance had been instilled in me early on. It was part of the immigrant experience. Men like my father, who came to this country virtually penniless, with neither prospects nor connections, learned that their best bet was always the one they placed on themselves. After all, in those days there were few government agencies to depend on, few social services, and certainly nothing like the social welfare system or the sense of entitlement we see in our country today. It is also worth noting that large corporations did not have the kind of influence they have today.

Men like my father and Manny Winrow understood that they had to be their own bosses simply to survive. Government help, such as subsidies, was not available so there was no reason for anyone to expect it. The entrepreneurial spirit was needed more than it probably is today; men like my father and Manny relied on that spirit to earn a living. However, as Winley-Morris grew, I eventually had to face the fact I could not be a one-man show. I was a family man with growing children and I wanted to spend more time with them. I was discovering, for the first time, that there really were only twenty-four hours in a day. And there was only so much I could do in those twenty-four hours. I also had to acknowledge that I had weaknesses in making business decisions. For instance, I always had trouble assessing the skills of the people I employed. That first became evident in some of the employees I chose to hire in the retail pharmacies I owned. And it remained a problem at Winley-Morris.

I have not always been proficient at putting the right people in the right positions. I have often gone with my gut when judging prospective employees and my gut has not always been right. It was seldom a question of the character or capability of the people I hired: it was, instead, a case of my trying to squeeze a square peg into a round hole.

And there were things I simply did not like to do. To be specific, I was reluctant to fire people who were underperforming. My instinct, always, was to give employees a second chance. As a result, some ended up staying in jobs they were unsuited for longer than they should have.

Of course, not all my personnel decisions were wrong. Some proved to be excellent choices for Winley-Morris. This is where Ted Wise and Dick MacKay enter the picture.

Theodore Sandy Wise, better known as Ted, was a native of British Columbia and, while he earned a BSc degree in pharmacy from the University of British Columbia, he was really a natural-born salesman. When he was still at university, he worked summers as a Fuller Brush salesman, a job he was successful at and that I think he would tell you had a significant influence on his future career in the pharmaceutical industry. Going door-to-door taught Ted that selling directly to the consumer could be a lot more productive and satisfying than standing behind a counter in a retail store waiting for customers to come to you. Ted came to Montreal to study marketing at McGill and his particular passion for that side of the business ended up serving him well since, at the time, his British Columbia pharmacy license was not recognized in Quebec. Here's Ted's version of how he ended up at Winley-Morris:

> I went to work for Ayerst Laboratories in 1955 when I arrived in
> Montreal and I stayed there four years. I didn't speak French,
> but I worked in the west end of the city where knowledge of
> French was not required in those days. That was possible in
> those days. But Morris must have heard about me somewhere

and he asked me to come to work for Winley-Morris as a salesman. I agreed because I knew Canada and I wanted to develop
some of the products at Winley-Morris for the national market.

Just a year later, Ayerst asked Ted to come back, making him the
kind of offer we both knew he could not turn down. Ayerst was going
to put Ted in charge of eight sales managers and expand his market
from national to worldwide. He was getting everything he could have
asked for. In fact, as soon as he told me about the job I told him there
was no way he could refuse it. What I said to him – and he remembers this clearly, I'm sure – was, "Take it for God's sake, Ted." But
then I added, "Come back to me one day." As it turned out, Ted's
opportunities at Ayerst, while significant, were limited. After working
there for the next six years, he was told, in so many words, that he
had gone about as far as he could at Ayerst. What accounted for this
Ted would probably not care to speculate on. But I can. Was it because he was Jewish? I suspect that had something to do with it.
While Ayerst, the largest Canadian-owned pharmaceutical company
at the time, employed Jews, mainly in the labs, there were not many
in the sales and marketing departments. In fact, there was only Ted.
Perhaps it is enough to say he was considered an outsider. That was
not the case at Winley-Morris, of course. There were no such limitations with us. Ted Wise came back to work for Winley-Morris and
some sixteen years later he and I became partners in a brand new venture. We started our business lives over by founding Pharmascience,
but that comes later.
    Richard "Dick" MacKay came to work for Winley-Morris in the
early 1960s, around the same time as Ted, and just as Ted took much
of the responsibility for sales and marketing off my hands, Dick freed
me from having to do the kind of administrative work I have never
been fond of. Dick also brought much needed structure to Winley-
Morris, helping me to develop company policy. So while I hired Ted
mainly to expand the company, I hired Dick to help me run it.
    Dick had been a salesman for Parke-Davis, which eventually be-
came part of Pfizer. His territory included the Jewish General Hospital and the chief pharmacist at the Jewish General, Sam Bagan, had
told me that Dick was a good guy looking to make a career change.
I think Dick was tired of being on the road all the time as a salesman.
At any rate, I was told that Dick would be an asset to Winley-Morris
and that was certainly true for a long time. What I first noticed about

him was that he combined an entrepreneurial spirit with the foresight of a visionary.

Dick did not have any more education in how to run a company than I did; like me, he learned on the job. But he had a knack for corporate structure and he quickly developed a corporate mentality. All of this came naturally to him, the way sales came naturally to Ted. Dick seemed to know, intuitively, that a proper pecking order was necessary in a growing company, an aspect of business I had frankly ignored. Before Dick, there were no titles at Winley-Morris. Once Dick grew into his role, he made it his goal to see that employees had clear job descriptions.

That included me. Hiring Ted and Dick gave Winley-Morris more depth as a company than it had had before. But, more important, it freed me to concentrate on finding and developing new products, which has always been the part of the business I am most passionate about. I also had more and more freedom to focus on my own vision for Winley-Morris, a vision that I believe made us unique in the industry. Our mission was not tied to how much profit we could make but to how we could bring better drugs to the market, even if that meant drugs targeted at small niche markets. Of course, I wanted to make money, but I knew that if I provided added value to my clients by having a better product to offer them, the financial returns would come. From a corporate point of view, I have always looked at business a bit backwards. Some people would probably say that I have always put the cart before the horse. For me, the product comes first, followed by its financial potential. Money, as Shawna pointed out, has always been a secondary objective for me. My primary objective, I suppose you could even call it a philosophy, was to help people by providing them with the drugs they needed. At Winley-Morris we were fortunate enough to be able to do just that. As far as I was concerned, there was nothing particularly noble or philanthropic about this approach to business, it simply made sense.

Ted Wise was a key figure in putting this approach into action. Working at Winley-Morris, he introduced numerous products to the Canadian market in the 1960s. Among them was the first commercial preparation of lithium carbonate, which we called Carbolith. To this day, Carbolith remains the drug of choice for manic-depression, now commonly referred to as bipolar disorder. There was also Cortenema, a hydrocortisone treatment for colitis, which is still on the market. Of course, not everything we introduced at Winley-Morris had enduring success. It is in the nature of the pharmaceutical business that innovative drugs make old drugs obsolete. You are always looking for newer products that will make things better, that will have fewer side effects, that will be easier to administer and achieve better compliance from patients. This is the nature of our business. It is what distinguishes it from other businesses. You are always on the lookout for the next big thing, even if it means improving or replacing a product that is already selling well for you. In a way, you are always in competition with yourself. Simply put, if you do not keep improving what you have, it is inevitable that someone else will. This kind of restlessness and experimentation is at the heart of the pharmaceutical business.

But even new products have their limitations, limitations you cannot always foresee. It is also true that even if they succeed, sometimes they are successful only for a limited time. Something else, something better, simpler, or cheaper comes along. Cytospray was a case in point.

In 1962, Roz and I decided to visit the Seattle World's Fair and I took the opportunity, once more, to mix business and pleasure. On the trip, I brought along two samples of a product called Cytospray – which came onto the market as a fixative used in cytology, the study of cells. Myron Pantzer of Panray Corporation had described Cytospray to me as a breakthrough in fixing slides for the Pap smear, a test routinely used in the diagnosis of cervical cancer. The problem at the time was that the usual fixative was made of a mixture of acetone and alcohol that caused frequent problems because it was extremely messy and awkward for both the doctors and the labs to use. Cytospray, which came in an easy-to-use two-ounce aerosol spray can, ended all the complaints that came with using the acetone-alcohol mixtures.

So before Roz and I arrived in Seattle, we made our way to the British Columbia Cancer Control Centre, the largest laboratory of its kind in Canada at the time, located on the grounds of the Vancouver General Hospital. The chief technician at the Centre told me that they were doing more than 100,000 tests a year. In fact, all the tests for the province were being done in that one facility. He also made it clear that he would be "very interested" in any product that could replace the alcohol-acetone fixative and would be more than happy to switch to my product if it proved to be a more effective option. I left the two samples of Cytospray I had bought and also had more samples sent from Montreal. Then Roz and I went on to Seattle. On my way back, I dropped in on that technician again to see what he thought. He was already sold. He enthusiastically endorsed Cytospray and recommended its use for the entire province. Indeed, for several years, Cytospray became the main fixation solution used in Pap smear tests across Canada.

Then a funny thing happened. It was discovered that ordinary women's hairspray worked just as effectively as our product and was, obviously, less expensive. You could get an eight-ounce can at the drugstore for 99 cents while a two-ounce can of Cytospray sold for something like $2.50. What would you choose? Obviously, the use of Cytospray plummeted. In fact, I only mention this story because it is a worthwhile lesson in how unpredictable the pharmaceutical business can be, as well as how the scientific process works through trial and error, often with surprising and unpredictable results.

The important thing to keep in mind, however, is that bringing Cytospray to market provided an important benefit to cytologists and physicians taking Pap smear specimens across the country. It made a difference to the quality of the specimens and to the way cytologists performed procedures. And it made a difference to physicians, for whom the procedure became clearer and easier.

◆

During Winley-Morris's growth spurt in the 1960s, I was keenly aware of the potential of generic drugs. Early on, the big drug companies had been inclined to do more than frown on anyone involved in manufacturing generic drugs. I can certainly attest to this – I have firsthand experience of being on the wrong side of their wrath.

One memorable example occurred in 1960, when two American pharmaceutical giants, Merck and Schering, got into a squabble over the patent for the drug Prednisone, a corticosteroid used to treat a variety of ailments. Prednisone was very new at the time and it marked a significant improvement over the first steroid on the market, Cortisone: it was a cleaner treatment, with fewer side effects. Because of the patent dispute, no one was in a position to determine who owned the drug. To my simple way of thinking, I figured if Merck and Schering could not figure out who owned the drug, then nobody owned it and I was free to work without much fear of being sued. Around that time, I came across an advertisement from the company Nysco, which was offering Prednisone tablets with patent pro-

tection. In other words, Nysco assumed the responsibility for ensur-
ing that there would be no infringement of anyone's patent and thus
covered any possibile liability we might have had. I started buying
Prednisone from them and brought it into Canada. Prednisone remains an effective treatment for everything from allergies to immuno-
logical disorders, from arthritis to cancer. It also happened to be
Winley-Morris's first major entry into the generic market. It would
not be our last.

I sold our tablets for $150 per 1,000, half the price being charged
by the major brands. I made $75 a bottle and also made it onto the
radar – and not in a good way – of the biggest pharmaceutical companies. Fortunately, the best they could do was to call me names: "pirate," to be exact. But while it bothered me initially to hear that kind
of thing said about me, it didn't bother me for long. I went right on
pursuing generic drugs. This was an important moment for the
generic drug industry because it revealed a significant chink in the ar-
mour of the multinationals: there was no way around the simple fact
that Prednisone was Prednisone. There was no difference between
what they were making, under their brand name, and what we were
selling. Still, their immediate reaction to losing business to companies
like Winley-Morris was to try to stop me from selling a generic version. Fortunately, their attempts didn't amount to much, an indication of their ultimate powerlessness. You can be sure that if I could
have been successfully sued I would have been.

A little-known fact about the generic industry in Canada – it had
an American father. Jules R. Gilbert, then in Toronto, established
Craig Pharmaceuticals with his partner, Bill Bell, but the partnership
did not last and Gilbert, on his own, set out to have the patent laws
governing drug manufacture and distribution changed in Canada. At
that time, American drug firms dominated the Canadian market and
eventually Canada's federal government, lobbied in large part by
Gilbert, looked into drug distribution in this country. The government report read: "The dominance of branches and subsidiaries of
United States drug firms and the widespread use in Canada of drug
products originated in the United States mean that drug trade in
Canada, in effect, operates under the United States patent system."
This report led to the passage, in 1969, of Bill C-102, which introduced "compulsory licensing." New legislation made it possible for
any company in Canada to produce a patented drug, paying a royalty
of four percent to the company that had introduced the drug. In other

words, it was compulsory for a company that introduced a new drug to license its distribution as a generic drug to a Canadian company that was prepared to pay the royalty. Suddenly, generic drugs were not only legal and protected by the Canadian government, companies like mine were being encouraged to delve into the generic market. This change dramatically altered the situation for Winley-Morris. The new legislation drew little public attention at the time, but those of us involved in distributing pharmaceuticals in Canada recognized that there were vast new opportunities. Medicare was not yet in place but was certainly on the horizon; once established, it would make the sale of generic drugs even more popular, widespread, and inevitable.

The passing of Bill C-102 also had a dramatic impact on how much Canadians paid for many of their medications, which proved to be much less than their neighbours south of the border were paying. Bill C-102 gave Canadians a break on prescription costs and opened the door for considerable growth among companies producing generic drugs in this country. This legislation made it possible for Canadian-owned generic companies not only to exist but to thrive.

In June 1958, I contacted Jules Gilbert and Winley-Morris became his distributor in Quebec and Newfoundland. I even formed a company to handle Gilbert's generic products, calling it Julius R. Gilbert (Quebec) Limited. The new company protected Winley-Morris from being sued and also made it possible for me to provide Gilbert with the sales force he badly needed in this region. But while we did very well, Gilbert was kept busy and broke, pouring his income into fees for patent lawyers. The multinationals bled him dry with patent infringement lawsuits and eventually his company went bankrupt. Gilbert's son-in-law, Fred Klapp, bought up the assets and ran a successful business developing creams and ointments under the label K-Line Pharmaceuticals. Later, he sold to Taro, which would become a major supplier of creams and ointments in both Canada and the United States.

Jules Gilbert lost his business, but, in the end, his cause was not lost. He was a bright, aggressive man, who changed the patent laws in Canada. He also paid the price for a number of us – Lesley Dan of Novopharm, Barry Sherman of Apotex, and me at Winley-Morris, ICN, and finally Pharmascience, not to mention all the other generic companies. Gilbert was a crusader and the Canadian public owes him a great debt because of his efforts to ensure that Canadians benefit from lower drug prices. The entire Canadian generic industry is also beholden to him for his unrivalled leadership. He opened the door for all of us. Had Jules Gilbert received the backing he needed – and should have had – it is also highly likely he would have become Canada's number one producer of generic drugs. Instead, by the beginning of the 1970s it began to look as if Winley-Morris was headed in that direction. We certainly had the advantage of being in on the ground floor of the soon-to-be burgeoning generic industry.

The little company I had started in 1953 while I was still a university student was bringing in a little over a million dollars in annual sales and was growing steadily. But life is an experiment, too – an unpredictable one. I would never have guessed that by 1971 Winley-Morris, the company into which I had poured my heart and soul, would no longer exist and, even more surprising, I would be the person responsible for its disappearance.

7

Seller's Remorse

Make it a rule of life never to regret and never to look back. Regret is an appalling waste of energy; you can't build on it. It's only good for wallowing in.

Katherine Mansfield

From the time I was ten going on eleven and hired as a delivery boy by Manny Winrow, I became aware that doing business is not just about money. And, as I would realize a decade later, neither is building a business. For accountants, dollars and cents, profit and loss, is the bottom line; it is music to their ears. For me, it is the dull stuff. This dollar-and-cents definition of a bottom line seldom takes into account what really matters in business – things like timing, luck, intuition, personality, and interpersonal relationships.

For instance, you just happen to bump into a doctor you are acquainted with standing in line at a downtown movie theatre and he gives you an unsolicited tip. He has no ulterior motive. He is just offering a word of friendly advice. Or you make a cold call to the flamboyant president of a company a continent away and the next thing you know he has flown in on his private jet to meet you and make you an offer that will change your life. How I decided to sell Winley-Morris, how I eventually got a part of it back, and how that part, renamed and re-envisioned as Pharmascience, would grow beyond my wildest dreams, is such a story.

◆

Happy campers. That is what we should have been. It is certainly what I expected I would be. On Wednesday morning, 3 March 1971, Roz and I flew to New York City to check into Manhattan's luxurious, landmark St. Regis Hotel. But I was in no position to enjoy the elegant surroundings. That morning, Roz and I met briefly with the bankers representing ICN, the company that was buying Winley-Morris. They presented us with papers, which I dutifully signed. In return, we collected our cheque and left New York the following morning.

I could not wait to distance myself from everything that had just taken place. I did not know it at the time but Roz understandably felt different. She was pregnant with our youngest daughter, Shawna, and had three small children at home, so I can see that this was an opportunity for her to relax a little. She would not have minded staying a few extra days at the St. Regis. She would have been fine doing some shopping at Saks Fifth Avenue. The thing is – she was right. We should have been overjoyed. After all, this decision was intended to set us and our family up for life. But along with the understanding that I had made my family secure came an unexpected feeling. If I had to try to identify what it was, what I was experiencing at that moment, it would be sadness, a vague unhappiness that overtook me suddenly and surprisingly. At the time, though, I chalked all this up to a combination of everything that had gone into my decision to sell Winley-Morris – namely, the previous two months of weighing pros and cons.

On the one hand, ICN or the International Chemical and Nuclear Corporation, based in Pasadena, California, very clearly appeared to be a company on the rise. With annual sales of $100 million, ICN may not have been a giant multinational but it was a company with big plans and it was run, I was about to discover, by a man with even bigger ambitions. That same man had also given me assurances that I was going to play a key role in ICN's future. From my vantage point, it looked like a bright, limitless future. In any case, I had agreed to the deal and ICN's potential was one of the main reasons I had agreed to it; it is also why I took part of the payment in stock, not cash. And while Winley-Morris was officially sold, unofficially I was going to continue to run my old company, or at least this new, expanded version of it. In fact, the moment I accepted ICN's cheque, I became president of a Canadian subsidiary of a multinational pharmaceutical company. Overnight, I was Big Pharma. It was the kind of position I had always dreamed of holding. During my next twelve years running ICN in Canada, there would be challenges, of course, but the position, at least until the last difficult months, would provide me with a great deal of satisfaction.

Even so, the decision to sell Winley-Morris had not been easy. That had become obvious a year earlier when ICN's president, Milan Panic, flew to Montreal in his private jet to meet me and offered to buy my company. I suppose I should have seen this offer coming. I should have known that a man like Panic does not show up at your doorstep seemingly out of the blue unless he has a very good reason. Just a few days before Panic and I met, he had sent a representative from his head office in California to review Winley-Morris's financial statements. I didn't think anything of this at the time since Panic and I had already begun what I believed to be the negotiations to establish Winley-Morris as the exclusive distributor of a new breakthrough drug ICN was developing. The drug was L-DOPA and it was being touted as a cure for Parkinson's disease. I expected ICN and Panic to do their due diligence as far as our relatively small Canadian company was concerned. I would have done the same in their place. I also understood that they wanted to reassure themselves that Winley-Morris was going to prove to be a sound business partner. What I did not know then was the kind of plans Panic had in mind for me and my company.

I also did not know what kind of man Panic was, one whose own tumultuous history had taught him to believe that he could accomplish anything as long as he set his mind to it. That history had included fighting Nazis, fleeing the communists, and founding a multinational company from scratch. Later, in the early 1990s, he served as prime minister of what was then called the Federal Republic of Yugoslavia. He also ran for president of Serbia in 1992 but ended up being defeated by Slobodan Milosevic, who would later lead his new country into a brutal civil war and eventually be convicted of war crimes.

Milan Panic remains one of the most charismatic figures I have ever met. He was born in 1929 in Belgrade, then the heart of the Balkan territories of Serbia, Croatia, and Slovenia. A teenager during the Second World War and the Nazi occupation, he joined the underground and served as a messenger for one of history's most celebrated and feared resistance fighters, Marshal Josip Broz Tito. After the war, Tito and the communists seized power in Yugoslavia and Panic waited impatiently for an opportunity to defect. His chance finally came in 1956 when he was visiting the Netherlands as part of the Yugoslavian Olympic cycling team. He literally cycled his way to freedom. This was a bold move on his part, but not an uncharacteristic one. Panic was and would always remain, in business and life, a risk-taker. Not long after he defected from the former Yugoslavia, he arrived in California and, in 1959, with a $200 stake, founded ICN in his Los Angeles garage.

Panic once said he was "born to fight," but the man I first met in 1970 was handsome and worldly – "mesmerizing" is the word Roz used to describe him. He was a charmer and he was certainly trying his best to charm me, at least until he revealed the real reason he had come to Montreal. The first time we met, over dinner at Ruby Foo's, Panic told me: "Morris, you should know that I'm not here because I'm interested in distributors for ICN. I'm here to buy your company. We'll give you enough money so you'll be financially taken care of. What's more, you'll be part of a very big organization."

I knew enough not to say anything immediately. Secretly, though, I was pleased. I could not help feeling flattered. For Winley-Morris, a relatively small Canadian pharmaceutical company, to be singled out and pursued by a company like ICN was obviously a feather in our cap. But I was not ready to let Panic know that, not yet. Even though we had just met, it did not take me long to figure out that his personality and mine were surprisingly similar in a lot of ways – with one significant exception. His willingness to take risks was far greater than my own. He was a man prepared to roll the dice. I cannot say that I always was.

Actually, in this way we complemented one another. Panic was an aggressive man, who wanted to win and win at all costs. He was also a man in a hurry. He could hardly wait to put his cards on the table. I also think he enjoyed the idea of catching me off guard and then studying my reaction. On the other hand, I was in no hurry. I had the advantage of being patient and the obligation to be cautious for the sake of my company and my family. I knew, for instance, I was not going to agree to anything until I consulted Roz.

So I looked Panic, my unexpected and eager suitor, in the eye and told him that Winley-Morris was not for sale. "I am thirty-nine years old," I said. "Why would I want to sell my company?"

I meant that. It was not in my nature to build something and then give it up. Nor was it in my nature to give up control of what I had built. Still, Panic had given me a lot to think about. There was the money, of course. His offer was generous if not overwhelming – it worked out to eighteen times Winley-Morris's net profit. But I was also thinking about how much my business could grow as a subsidiary of ICN. The question I had begun to ask myself was, what would be a better future for the Goodman family: going it alone or being a part of a multinational? One thing I knew: that night Roz and I would have a lot to talk about.

It is likely I never would have heard of ICN or Milan Panic if it were not for the drug L-DOPA, still the drug of choice in the treatment of Parkinson's disease. In 1970, a little over a year before the sale of Winley-Morris, I was waiting in line outside a movie theatre when I bumped into Dr. Arthur Schwartz, who was affiliated with Maimonides Hospital, a leading geriatric care centre in Montreal. He recognized me and came over and the first word out of his mouth, maybe even before hello, was L-DOPA. He said, "L-DOPA. Morris, get hold of L-DOPA. We're doing research on it and it's a great, great drug."

That meeting, the pure coincidence of it, highlights the importance of personal relationships. Arthur Schwartz may not have known me well, but he knew me well enough to know that I would jump at the chance to learn more about L-DOPA, which was already being referred to as a "wonder drug." So here he was giving me a tip, the kind of tip, as he was well aware, given Winley-Morris's reputation, that was right up our alley. I knew, for instance, that there were only about 300 neurologists in Canada, which made this the kind of niche specialty area Winley-Morris was well established to service. We knew we could develop relationships with a small group of doctors. It was not like approaching 20,000 general practitioners across the country.

Besides, the chance to narrow in on a niche market was precisely what we were looking for. It was also an opportunity to introduce a new and effective drug to a suffering community – people with Parkinson's. I was keeping up with my reading in the field and therefore was well aware that several of the leading medical journals as well as the media had begun to trumpet L-DOPA as "a miracle cure" for Parkinson's.

For his part, Dr. Schwartz had begun performing clinical tests on L-DOPA with his Parkinson patients at Maimonides and he was seeing remarkable results. So were other doctors. Ted Wise recalled the time he was in Saskatchewan and had talked to one Parkinson sufferer who had been treated with L-DOPA. Ted had seen a video of this particular patient before meeting him. The patient had been living in his wheelchair, struggling in vain to get food up to his mouth. Tragically, he was shaking so badly he could not do even that. But the man Ted met that day was steady. He was standing on his own, talking and, in Ted's words, "thanking the heck out of me." Ted, meanwhile, had to ask him about the way he was looking at the nurses as they went by. He wondered out loud if L-DOPA just might be an aphrodisiac. Back then, there were legends to that effect. But the patient told Ted, "Hell no. It's nothing like that. You see, before the drug my mind was entirely focused on doing things like eating on my own. You saw it in the video," he went on. "I had to concentrate. Before L-DOPA, if a naked woman had walked by, I wouldn't have taken note. But now I'm standing and looking. What's more, if I get the chance, one day I'll be pinching."

The 1990 film *Awakenings*, starring Robert De Niro and Robin Williams and based on the book by renowned neurologist and author Oliver Sacks, dramatizes the early effect L-DOPA had on the most severe cases, on people who had been in a kind of suspended animation for decades. The problem, then as now, is that the drug would not prove to be the cure it was originally hoped to be.

Its effectiveness does not last. The body eventually develops a tolerance to L-DOPA, a fact dramatically and poignantly depicted in *Awakenings*.

However, in 1970, the potential for L-DOPA to help patients no other drug had was undeniably exciting. In medicine and the pharmaceutical business, this was the kind of breakthrough that is the equivalent of being struck by lightning. A synthesis of amino acids, L-DOPA replaces dopamine in the brain. Dopamine is a neurotransmitter and if there is not enough of it going through your system, the result is Parkinson's. The Swedish scientist Arvid Carlsson, who in 2000 won the Nobel Prize for his work with L-DOPA, had begun his research on the drug half a century earlier. In 1950, he had discovered that administering L-DOPA to animals with Parkinsonian-like symptoms caused a reduction in the intensity of their symptoms.

In 1970, two decades later, I followed up on Arthur Schwartz's tip and started looking into L-DOPA. Basically, I did this by picking up the telephone. This was routine for me – making cold calls, trying to secure Canadian rights. It was the kind of detective work I have always enjoyed. Eventually, I discovered that ICN, based in Irvine,

California, was the only company in the United States with access to a significant supply of L-DOPA. (ICN had secured the drug from a company in Japan.) So I made a cold call to ICN's president, Milan Panic. He did not get back to me for three days. I remember I had to give his secretary hell just to get him to return my call. When he finally did, I told him I was looking for exclusive distribution rights for L-DOPA in Canada. In fact, it was the potential I saw in L-DOPA that became another reason, another entry on the pro side of the list, behind my decision to sell Winley-Morris. I knew my little company did not have sufficient resources to pursue the drug's research and development and eventual marketing. I knew Winley-Morris was just too small to fulfill the potential of what was looking more and more like a "wonder drug." Once Winley-Morris was bought and had become ICN Canada, I began distributing L-DOPA capsules, for research purposes, to Dr. Andre Barbeau at the Montreal Clinical Research Institute. Dr. Barbeau was regarded as "the father of L-DOPA in Canada." It was an exciting time.

But, as it turned out, ICN was also too small for L-DOPA. When, in 1973, the drug was finally approved by health authorities for sale in Canada and the United States, we were out-marketed by Hoffman-La Roche, one of the largest international pharmaceutical companies around. We had been able to compete with Hoffman-La Roche in selling L-DOPA to research institutions, but we could not match their sales and marketing resources. My hope had been that the doctors we had been supplying with the research capsules would stay with us. But we could not give the neurologists the research support they needed after the drug was approved. Nor did we have the promotional muscle to convince doctors to prescribe our product. Whatever the reasons, it was evident in a few years that L-DOPA was not going to become a part of the future for ICN that I had imagined when I sold Winley-Morris.

But I am getting ahead of myself. Flashback to that night when I met Panic in 1970. What do I remember? I remember leaving Ruby Foo's with a swelled head and a tough decision to make. If Panic had not exactly made me an offer I could not refuse, he had made me an offer I could certainly not refuse to think about. Theoretically, I would be financially secure. This was the case Roz and her mother would make on behalf of selling the company when I consulted them. They were making sense. We all came from a background where this kind of lump sum understandably seemed like too much to pass up.

The fact is that the economic background you come from will inevitably determine whether you are inclined to accept an offer and be satisfied with it or refuse it. Still, I have always taken my wife's advice very seriously and I had, over the course of our marriage, learned to do the same with her mother.

Edythe Druker and I enjoyed a close relationship. She was a woman I could not help but admire. Brought up in the little town of Erickson in Manitoba, Edythe Druker, neé Donér, was the daughter of pioneer parents who had come to Canada from Odessa, Russia, in the late 1800s. They were the first Jewish family to settle in a Swedish-Canadian community and had begun their business career by owning a successful general store. Edythe's father, Abraham Doner, was an entrepreneur who had acquired a license from the Canadian government to build a lodge in Manitoba's Riding Mountain National Park, commonly known as Clear Lake. The lodge became a popular meeting place for young Jewish singles from Winnipeg. The Doners became a prominent and educated Manitoba family. In fact, Edythe's uncle, Fred Doner, was one of the key organizers of the 1919 Winnipeg General Strike, which was sparked by dangerous working conditions and low wages in the metal and building trades in the city following the First World War. The strike lasted a little over a month and saw 30,000 workers walk off the job. It was finally ended after a violent intervention by the RCMP: two strikers were killed and thirty more injured on a day that came to be known as "Bloody Saturday." Part of the significance of the strike, however, was that one of its leaders, J.S. Wordsworth, would go on to found the party that later become known as the NDP or the National Democratic Party, currently the loyal opposition in Ottawa.

Edythe was a tough-minded, smart, and determined woman. In the 1930s, when she was still single, she had had high-profile jobs with companies like Canadian Pacific Railways and American Can Corp. She was well travelled and sophisticated and when she came to Montreal, she got herself a lovely apartment on Bernard Street. Later, after she married Roz's father, Joseph Druker, she ran her own successful motel, Willow Beach, across the U.S. border on Route 9 in Plattsburgh, New York, at a time when it was rare for a woman to do that kind of thing. All in all, she was a good person to go to for business advice. At the same time, I knew selling Winley-Morris was going to be much more than a simple business decision.

Roz was also advising me to sell Winley-Morris. She had always been a sounding board for me, but this was, far and away, the toughest decision we had yet to face as a couple. "At twenty-eight, I don't think I was mature enough to understand what Morris was going through," Roz recently recalled, adding:

> The fact is selling Winley-Morris did give us a better quality of life. I was very happy during those years. It gave us more of a normal home. Morris was president of ICN Canada and worked above and beyond the call of duty.
>
> But, even so, we had much more stability. We had weekends and holidays free. And we travelled more. But I know that if Morris doesn't exactly blame me and my mother for talking him into selling Winley-Morris, he does blame himself for listening to us. He has great regrets about selling to ICN. He would be Apotex today, the number one generic company in Canada. By the way, Barry Sherman, founder and owner of Apotex, worked for Morris at ICN. On the other hand, Morris learned a tremendous amount at ICN. He was thrust into an international milieu.
>
> What did he know, a kid from the streets? What did he know about corporate structure? Still, Pharmascience is now the number three generic company in Canada and, of course, he believes in his heart of hearts that if he hadn't sold Winley-Morris when he did he would be first. And I believe in my heart that he's right.

Frankly, I am not sure if Roz is right about what she refers to as my regrets. Regret is too strong a word. I certainly do not spend a lot of time thinking about that period in my life, at least not in what I would call an emotional way. But I can analyze my decision in retrospect and see that I was on the ground floor of generic drugs just as the industry was taking off in this country. My association with Jules Gilbert, the father of the generic industry, attests to that. I understood the generic business. I could see changes coming in Canadian laws, a change like 1969's Bill C-102 that introduced "compulsory licensing." Compulsory licenses were inevitably going to make an enormous difference in the generic business. What stung, I suppose, was the knowledge that I was a pioneer in generics, going back to the 1950s, going back to those days of my being called a "pirate." But I did not get the chance to take advantage of the situation, of everything I knew and learned, because of the sale of Winley-Morris. I lost my chance to be first in the country in generic drugs. I saw the opportunities and gave them all to ICN, but as it turned out, they did not want them.

The decision to sell Winley-Morris was always going to be a complicated and difficult one. I understood that accepting Panic's offer might make it possible for me to live in two worlds. Two good worlds was the way I thought of it at the time. I saw this offer as a chance to have my cake and eat it too. The money Panic was putting on the table was going to provide my family with financial security – the kind of security I did not have with Winley-Morris since back then all my money was tied up in the company.

But there were other considerations, important ones that had less to do with money. With ICN, I would have the opportunity to be involved in the kind of research I knew I could never do at Winley-Morris. I was proud of my company, a company that I had spent my entire adult life building. But I also thought that, compared to ICN, Winley-Morris's future was limited.

After some two decades of building Winley-Morris on my own, I was also beginning to realize how alone I was feeling. I needed to work with people who had greater vision and know-how than I did. I also began to feel that there was another way to run the business and make it prosper. I liked the idea of being connected to others, especially others with a greater international vision and more corporate experience. All in all, the decision to sell was a practical one. Maybe, though, it was too practical.

Because, if all these things were the pros, there was one big con on my list that I was having a hard time ignoring. It would linger even after I sold the company. Winley-Morris was my baby, our baby, Roz's and mine. This probably explains why that cheque we found ourselves in possession of on that March day in 1971 at the St. Regis Hotel, that substantial cheque we had anticipated would make us so happy, seemed to be doing the exact opposite. At least, I know it was making me unhappy. As Roz has already mentioned, she would not have minded doing a little additional shopping and staying a few more nights in a luxury hotel.

I am not a person who gets depressed or dwells on the past, so this kind of sadness and regret were unexpected feelings for me, feelings I was not used to. The best plan I could think of was to deposit the cheque as soon as possible, but it seems I was destined to think about our decision a little while longer anyway. When Roz and I got home to Montreal, the city was completely snowed in. The streets were not going to be cleared for a few days. So for a few more days, my sadness remained. All I could think about was: here we have this cheque and we are losing interest on it daily, lots of interest. But I am a problem-solver, so I set about solving this immediate problem. I got my hands on a ski-doo – you could order them then with a driver, just like taxis – and somehow I made it to the bank to deposit the cheque.

8

The Writing on the Wall

Entrances are wide; exits are narrow.
Jewish proverb

It is only in retrospect that we can imagine dividing our lives into chapters. The reality of how a person's story unfolds is never that clear-cut. The twelve years I spent as chief operating officer of ICN Canada is not as easy to categorize as a separate phase of my life as it seems looking back. In fact, it was all part of a continuum. A learning curve, too, as Roz would say. As it turns out, I learned a lot during my time with ICN – about business and about myself.

First, there was an adjustment to make: I had to go from being the single person responsible for everything that happened at Winley-Morris to being a smaller part of a much larger operation. At ICN, this transition was more gradual, more seamless than most people would guess. Still, there were moments at ICN when the sharp contrast between all those years I had absolute control over the day-to-day operations of Winley-Morris and the years I spent running ICN Canada on behalf of ICN Corporate are hard, now, to overlook.

For instance, when ICN lost out on the market for L-DOPA, I had an early indication that the size and reach of this new company I was now part of was not as unlimited as I had initially imagined and hoped. One reason for selling Winley-Morris had been to do bigger things in the pharmaceutical world, in particular the world of research. So this early setback was a disappointment and a kind of foreshadowing that there are always limits. Even in the world of what is now routinely called Big Pharma, everything is relative. There is often someone else who is bigger, more connected, more farsighted, and more willing to take risks than you are.

Similarly, my hope that ICN would develop a breakthrough anti-viral miracle drug called Ribavirin disappeared like soap bubbles after I sold Winley-Morris. The promise offered by Ribavirin was one of the incentives – one of the top pros on my pro and con list – that had led me to sell Winley-Morris to Milan Panic. Before my deal with Panic was finalized in March of 1971 I visited ICN headquarters in Irvine, California, located in the now famously affluent Orange County. (Incidentally, Canadians were buying property there at the time.) I witnessed first-hand how much research was being devoted to Ribavirin and I could not help but be impressed. In this, I was hardly alone.

ICN's plan, or, more specifically, Milan Panic's plan, for Ribavirin should not have come as a surprise to anyone. After all, he was a man used to taking on enormous, seemingly impossible challenges. When I first met him in the early 1970s, the impossible challenge he had set for himself was to create a new molecule that was going to revolutionize the market for anti-viral drugs – he was determined to come up with an effective treatment for colds. He didn't have a lot riding on what was clearly a long shot – he had everything riding on it. He was betting ICN's future on Ribavirin. He had founded and funded the ICN Research Institute based, in large part, on the work of Dr. Roland Robins, a researcher at the University of Utah, and, in particular, on Robins's work with anti-viral agents. Panic's thinking was that he needed some kind of incredible breakthrough to attract interest, both scientific and financial, to ICN. He knew that in order to get the financial community to back him in his dream of building a worldwide multinational company he had to fill a gap in the marketplace – in this case, a legendary gap that no one else had come close to filling.

Ribavirin was seriously being considered as the drug to cure the common cold. In the pharmaceutical business, the Common Cold is the equivalent of the Holy Grail. The possibility, if not probability, that there is a single drug out there that will one day vanquish the human race's countless bouts of sniffles and congestion, and that that drug is just waiting to be discovered and introduced to a mass market, has always been too enticing to overlook. For starters, finding a cure for the common cold had the capacity to make a person a multibillionaire overnight. That kind of reward was bound to make a lot of people, especially brokers on Wall Street, overlook a whole host of risks and pitfalls. Wall Street was, as a consequence, quick to come on board with Panic and Ribavirin. Why wouldn't it be? You have to realize that this grand plan of Panic's appealed to me and to others precisely because of its grandiosity. In our world, this kind of ambition and foresight are positives, not negatives. There was the real possibility that there was something miraculous being developed here. Indeed, anyone interested in new science and new breakthroughs was interested in keeping an eye on what happened with Ribavirin and, by extension, ICN.

It also needs to be said that Panic had a lot to offer his investors and me as a partner. He had the basis of an ongoing business, as well as a research program and the backing of the financial community. It was also the era of mergers and acquisitions and Panic was buying up companies right and left. By March of 1971, that included Winley-Morris.

Needless to say, ICN did not have the cure for the common cold. At least, Ribavirin was not it. But it was also not the last I would hear of this drug and its usefulness. Its resiliency, in particular, would keep surprising me. Some twenty years later, combined with interferon, it would prove to be an effective treatment for Hepatitis C, a surprising development that ended up saving ICN from certain bankruptcy and rejuvenating Panic as a force to be reckoned with in the pharmaceutical business. And, a few years ago, Ribavirin came back onto my radar screen, though this time more directly and even more intriguingly. But I will get to that later.

There were other early indications that ICN's overall corporate mindset was going to be hard to reconcile with the vision I had for our Canadian branch. I was dealing with the kind of money restraints and oversights I had never had to deal with at Winley-Morris. I no longer had the last word on financial decisions. So while it is true that we at ICN Canada accumulated more compulsory licenses for generic drugs than any other Canadian company during the time I was running Canadian operations – between 1971 and 1982 – Panic was essentially uninterested in generics. And while I was as keen as Panic to pursue breakthrough drugs like L-DOPA and Ribavirin, I also understood there had to be a balance between generic and specialty drugs. But Panic and ICN International had no real vision of how to maximize sales or of the profitability of generics at the level we should or could have achieved at ICN Canada. (I was a pioneer in the generic industry; I knew it well, though even I underestimated its potential.) As a result, the parent company did not provide ICN Canada with the capital we needed to exploit all the licenses we had obtained for generic drugs. What it may have come down to was that Panic, in order to succeed with Wall Street, had to sell dreams along with drugs; my main interest was selling drugs.

Another glimpse of what the future held for me in this new corporate environment was evident early on when Panic purchased Empire Laboratories, a Canadian company owned by Barry Sherman and Joel Ulster. Empire became part of ICN Canada and Barry ended up working for me for six months. Shortly after, he got into an argument with some of the people at the corporate head office in California and one day I got a call from California. I do not know exactly what went on there – I assumed he got into some sort of conflict with the people there – but I was told to fire him. I went to Barry and told him about the phone call. He said, "Morris, don't worry about firing me, I quit."

He left ICN and started Apotex, where he followed the same program I had instituted at ICN Canada, only he did not have the restraints that were being put on me. Apotex would eventually become a powerhouse and end up beating us royally in the generic marketplace. It soon became, and has remained, the number one generic company in Canada.

Another day I will never forget is 22 February 1976. I was due to sign a new agreement with Stiefel Laboratories, with whom I had had a long-term relationship. Back in the 1950s, Stiefel had been the first agency we represented at Winley-Morris. But after I sold Winley-Morris to ICN, Stiefel began to express some concerns about being represented in Canada by a multinational. As a matter of fact, I had already been approached by Stiefel president Werner Stiefel about leaving ICN and coming to work for his company. But I had no intention of doing that and the subject was dropped or so I thought at the time. As a result, when it came time to renew our agreement, I decided to take a pass on traveling to New York to sign the verbally agreed upon contract renewal for an additional five years. Instead, I sent my right hand man, Dick MacKay, in my place. Dick had been an integral part of the business at Winley-Morris and was a vice-president at ICN Canada, working alongside me. Indeed, Panic had taken a particular liking to Dick and was grooming him for bigger things within the company. As an example, he had been sent to Harvard to do a specialized business course, which ICN paid for.

All of this begins to explain why I was completely unprepared for what happened next. Dick returned from his meeting with Stiefel, walked into my office, and told me he was leaving ICN to take the job Stiefel had offered me earlier. He said, "I'm quitting as of today."

I was in shock and was hurt. I also understood, as Dick explained to me at the time, that if I had not sold Winley-Morris to ICN, Stiefel would have continued with me, happily renewing their contract. But while Stiefel had a long-time personal relationship with me, they had no such relationship with ICN. Instead, Stiefel saw ICN as a big, public, impersonal corporation, one to which they owed no loyalty. I also understood some of Dick's frustrations. He wanted to build ICN Canada, and by the late 1970s, that was becoming more and more difficult to do under ICN corporate restraints.

Dick's announcement meant that he had signed an agreement with Stiefel and was going to take over their Canadian operation. It also made me wonder – if I had decided to go to that meeting in New York to renew our deal with Stiefel, would Stiefel have reneged on our verbal agreement? I am convinced they would not have. But I had taken the renewal for granted and this was the consequence.

Still, the new job was an undeniably great opportunity for Dick. Stiefel was very generous to him. In addition to becoming Canadian CEO, he received twenty-five percent of the company, no money down on his part. For me, however, that day remains the worst one I have experienced in my working life. It is possible that Dick now believes that his leaving should not have been that much of a surprise to me, but the fact is, it was. So much so I offered him the presidency of ICN Canada when he told me he was leaving to work for Stiefel.

But days like this notwithstanding, and despite having to adjust to the frustrations and politicking that came with being part of the corporate world, it would be misleading to say that the twelve years I spent at ICN Canada were unhappy ones. In fact, I had a good life and a stable one. As Roz already pointed out, our daily life was more normal than it had been during my years of building Winley-Morris. We took more family holidays and I spent more time with the kids, which made everyone happy. Roz is right when she says that while I still thought of ICN Canada as my business, it became easier for me to detach myself from it. My mindset had changed. There was less pressure in the job for me, at least in the early years. During those early years, it all came down to a simple question, one

I would actually end up asking myself from time to time, "what else do you want?" I did not need a private jet or a yacht. What would I do with a yacht? I can't even swim properly.

All of which raises another question: did I see the end of my career at ICN Canada coming? Was the writing on the wall? Or, perhaps, more precisely, when did I see the writing on the wall? I would like to say I saw it all along, but I honestly cannot claim to be that smart. The truth is I am convinced I would have stayed on at ICN Canada and done so happily if circumstances had not started to change in the late 1970s, and even then if they had not begun to change so dramatically.

For most of my time at ICN Canada, Milan Panic was a hands-off boss. He had no reason not to be: during the period of the early 1970s, ICN and ICN Canada were both growing, the former by acquisitions and mergers, the latter by internal growth. From 1971 to 1982, my entire time at ICN, ICN Canada grew from a company doing a little more than one million dollars in business annually to a $15 million enterprise. Ironically, that may have been the beginning of my problems.

I have already pointed out that business was, regrettably, not a part of the education my colleagues and I received at the University of Montreal's Faculty of Pharmacy. Then again, there were some things about business I could never have learned in any school. I could only learn them by experience and my last few years, particularly my last few months with ICN, provided me with a crash course in how upside-down the corporate world can sometimes be. For instance, in business what sometimes looks, in the short term, like failure can turn out to be success and vice versa. I was also about to learn that you can be too successful, the tough lesson of my final months working for Milan Panic. While our fortunes at ICN Canada were climbing, our parent company's fortunes, and Panic's, were declining – precipitously by my final year with the company. From $100 million the year after Panic bought Winley-Morris, the company's sales fell to $40 million. This change had a personal impact on me: remember, when I sold Winley-Morris, two-thirds of my payment was in cash, the other third in stocks. At that time an ICN share was worth $23 a share; when I finally sold my stock it was worth $4 a share. The truth is that I have not trusted the stock market since university, when I received a tip to invest in a mining stock called Tache Lake. It was my first venture into high-risk investing and perhaps my most instructive one. You see, Tache Lake was a hot commodity, a sure thing, or so I was told at the time. But, as with all stock market tips, especially sure things, what Tache Lake really was was a formula for disaster. The message here should have been clear to me: do not believe that stocks are always going to go up. In the end, I am guessing I lost only a couple of hundred dollars on Tache Lake, but I was barely out of my teens at the time and that seemed like a fortune. My experience with the rapid decline of ICN's once valuable stock was just a sobering reminder that this was a mistake I had made before.

When compared to the decline of the rest of ICN, not to mention the failure of Panic's idea of building a top-level multinational company, the success I was having at ICN Canada ended up working to my disadvantage. By 1982, ICN and Panic were hemorrhaging cash. Panic was understandably desperate and he began to look to our flourishing little operation in Canada as a last chance to bolster his business. Initially, he entertained the idea of selling ICN Canada. He was being squeezed from all sides and we were one of the most attractive commodities he had.

Which explains the arrival of a representative from the German branch of the pharmaceutical multinational giant Schering AG. Panic was trying to get an idea of what he could get for his Canadian subsidiary and this representative, based in Berlin, was there to assess the company. Meanwhile, I remember calling Roz to tell her that I wanted to invite the representative to our home for dinner. After all, there was a chance I would be working for him in the very near future. Roz said okay. It seemed like a thoughtful as well as a shrewd gesture. After all, really, what could go wrong?

Well, we had not counted on my youngest daughter, Shawna, who must have been around six at the time, walking into our dining room to meet our VIP guest. Shawna could not have looked sweeter or more innocent in her pigtails. I introduced our visitor and explained to her that he was from Berlin. She asked, "Where is that, Daddy?" I told her Germany. At which point, she put her arm in the air, clicked her heels together, and gave our guest the sieg heil salute. I could not believe my eyes. I was embarrassed and said, "Shawna, where did you get that?" "Daddy, that's from *Hogan's Heroes*," she replied with a childlike innocence, as if nothing could be more obvious. It was a lesson in the effect media like television has, especially on children. In any case, our guest was not amused.

In the end, Panic decided not to sell ICN Canada. Instead, he decided to take as much cash out of the company as he could. I understood his dilemma – he was like a drowning man grabbing at anything he could in order to stay afloat – but that does not mean I liked being the short-term solution to his long-term problem. He had already begun to isolate me inside my own company by firing my closest employees – Betty Speevak, my secretary, George Montgomery, even Ted Wise. Eventually, Panic sent a representative from his U.S. operation, a man by the name of Von Stein, to oversee the company and effectively take control of it.

For my part, Panic expressly told me to do nothing. On the one hand, he did not want me to leave the company. On the other hand, he wanted to make sure I was neutralized. This was corporate hardball. Panic had, because of his own difficulties, begun to distrust me. Meanwhile, I was concerned that he intended to drain the company of its cash, which would eventually put ICN Canada into bankruptcy, something that already happened to a number of ICN subsidiaries. However, in our case, the Canadian banks would not let ICN move forward with this strategy. The Canadian banking system then had what is called covenance: because ICN owed money to the bank, the bank was making it clear that money could not be taken out of the country without its approval. Panic also began to become paranoid and seemed to believe that I was colluding with the bank against him, which was utterly untrue.

Panic had already told me to take Roz on a trip around the world. Of course, I was not about to do that. It was increasingly clear to me that I was expected, at the very least, to take my paycheque and stay in my office with the door locked. And do what? What did they think I was going to do? Bring my train set in and play by myself? This went on for only a few weeks, but it was a stressful period. Mainly, though, it was irritating. I knew I would not be able to go on in this kind of limbo much longer, so I made a decision that involved my showing up at ICN's head office in California for a monthly meeting, even though I was, for all intents and purposes, no longer in charge of the Canadian branch of the company. At the meeting, I made some remarks, quite deliberately, and quite loudly, which were correctly interpreted by everyone present, Panic included. I made it as obvious as I could that I was unhappy with the situation I had been put in. Head office got the message, loud, clear, and face-to-face, that I was not going to do what they wanted. I was not going to sit around and do nothing all day. I was not going to take money for doing nothing either. That is not in my character. So Panic decided there was no need for me to be part of the company any longer. He told one of his people that "it was time for Morris to leave."

I believe Panic knew that in forcing me out, he was in the wrong. But he probably believed he had no choice. He could not afford to keep me – and not just because he was paying a salary to someone who was not being allowed to do anything. I had become a voice of dissent in the company. I was telling him things he did not like hearing, certainly not with his business in as much trouble as it was. Of course, by that point I could not stand being there either. So I precipitated the break.

In 1972, I had bought a Winnipeg company, Sabra Pharmaceuticals, and I had moved the owner, Jack Kay, and his family to Montreal to work for ICN Canada. During this transitional period, as I was preparing to leave ICN, Jack got a call from Barry Sherman at Apotex asking Jack to come work for him. He came running into my office to ask my advice. I told him, "Jack, Barry is smart. If I were you I would go work for him, but you won't do it because you know I'm leaving and you want to become president of ICN." He said, "You still don't know me." He left and became second-in-command at Apotex and he is still there.

I left ICN Canada the day I was fired. I was fifty-two years old and I was walked out of my office by the company's comptroller. He apologized to me, but I knew he was just doing his job. "Don't worry about it," I told him. "I understand." Looking back, I did not feel as bad about this departure as I probably should have. For one thing, I understood that it was not personal; it was the system. For another, it brought to a head what I really wanted. To move on. I was not about to sit around and do nothing so, in a sense, this last day came as a relief; it also brought me down to earth. I ceased being an employee of ICN on 27 May 1982. It had become absolutely clear to me that ICN was not my company and never had been.

Incidentally, I never had a contract with ICN. I could have left the day after I sold Winley-Morris and gone out and started a new company. And he could have fired me the day after he bought the company. It was funny – even as Panic and I were about to go our separate ways, it was impossible to deny the fact that we liked and respected each other. I always knew he had the foresight, the vision, what I would call the jazz, I did not have. As I said, we complemented each other. He was the risk-taker, I was the cautious one.

Milan Panic and I would remain in each other's lives. In 2006, he came up to Montreal from New York to attend my seventy-fifth birthday party. He gave a speech and spoke about everything he had learned from me in the time he had known me. He was paying tribute, really, to the way I had managed to balance my family life with my work life. That was a quality he admired.

9

Fresh Start

Even if you are on the right track, you'll get run over if you just sit there.
                                                                    Will Rogers

Confidence is relative. And while it is true that I have always considered myself a confident person, the difference between the man I was in 1971 when, at the age of thirty-nine, I sold my company to Milan Panic and the man I was, twelve years later, when I left ICN Canada, was enormous. In fact, I suspect if I had been more confident in 1971, I would never have sold Winley-Morris. Of course, if things had not gone downhill in my last year at ICN, I might not have left there. I guess I will really never know. But I did know, in 1983, that I was ready to open a new chapter in my life. And this time around I had no doubt that whatever I ultimately decided to do, I was going to do it my way. There is nothing like being fired to make a person reflect on what really matters and for me that meant sticking to my vision. That resolve would be the determining factor in my next undertaking.

The notion of holding to that vision began immediately, with the severance package I received from ICN. It was a fair deal, which included my purchasing a part of ICN business that Panic did not want. I received my severance cheque and then turned around and wrote a cheque of my own, buying some OTC (over the counter) preparations from ICN as well as ICN's private label vitamin business. Purchasing the latter meant I would be producing vitamins that would be sold under pharmacies' private labels.

Incidentally, Panic was not obliged to sell me anything. But, as we were both aware, none of what had transpired between us was personal. Neither of us had any reason to be spiteful or bitter. I understood why Panic had forced me out – he was fighting for his business survival – and he understood that it had been wrong for him to try to put me in a cage while he set about making changes I could not live with.

It helped, of course, that during this transitional period I was looking toward the future, focusing on a fresh start. I recommend this strategy to everyone who has had such a setback. Simply put, just get on with things – on to the next challenge. "Next" is a great word, full of potential and possibility. And, with that in mind, I started my next business the day I left ICN.

That business was selling private-label vitamins, which would serve as a foundation for any future businesses I intended to start. There was nothing flashy about vitamins, but I knew they would keep me afloat while I looked for new product lines. This proved to be the case and then some. Our new company, Dominion Pharmacal, was more profitable for me personally in its first year than my last year at ICN had been, including salary and bonus. (Dominion Pharmacal would soon be merged into Pharmascience, though it remains a trading name.) Either I had underestimated the vitamin business while I was at ICN or I had been seriously underpaid.

Another thing that made starting Pharmascience easier than it might have been was the fact that I was able to reconnect with my old friend and former employee Ted Wise. Ted and I had always worked well together, which is another way of saying our personalities were complete opposites. He was a people-person and a gifted salesman. If, at Winley-Morris, ICN Canada, and, later, Pharmascience, I was the inside force of the company – focusing on creating new products – Ted was the outside face.

One of his more impressive accomplishments came when he was in Frobisher Bay in the 1960s introducing Parasal-INH and other tuberculosis medications to the hospital treating the Inuit population. He was having minimal success until he realized the Inuit "did not like a white pill," as Ted put it at the time. "So we manufactured the pills in yellow, brown, red. Now that's what I call niche marketing." I am afraid there was also another reason, a more practical and disconcerting one, for introducing different coloured pills. The population was largely illiterate at that time and could not read the directions on the label. Colour coding made it easier for them to be sure they were taking the right medication.

By the time I was asked to leave ICN Canada, Ted, who had been my executive vice-president, had been gone a little less than a year. His dismissal from the company had been particularly unpleasant. If Ted was asked he would tell you that Mr. Von Stein, the representative Panic sent to take over ICN Canada from me, was out to get him from the start. Why? Ted was convinced it was because he had the nicest office and, perhaps more importantly, because that office was right across from mine. Von Stein did not like the fact that Ted was always going back and forth to meet with me. He worried that we were too close – literally and figuratively. As a consequence, Ted returned from a sales trip to find that the locks on the door to his office had been changed and he was being ordered to leave the building.

But Ted had a knack for rebounding no matter what circumstances he found himself in – that had been true at Ayerst, Winley-Morris, and ICN – and as soon as he was forced out of ICN, he was up and running a new business, developing specialty pharmaceuticals. This was, in a way, the beginning of Pharmascience. It was a modest start. Ted was running the company out of his home in Chomedey, Laval. Here is how Ted remembered that time:

> ICN fired Morris's long-time secretary, Betty Speevak, around the same time they fired me. So I hired Betty to work with me in my home. I was doing everything there, including hiring a sales force. I remember I bought two Brother typewriters. I also remember my wife had no intention of working for me or even being around while I was working so she got herself a job. She would leave the house at 8:30 a.m. and Betty would come in at 9:00 a.m. Wouldn't you know that a concerned neighbour called that same evening to talk to my wife about this unusual situation. Specifically about this new lady who was coming in once my wife was gone and the coast was supposedly clear. I'm telling you, I acquired quite the reputation.

Before I left ICN, Ted and I had not made any explicit plans to work together in the future, but we stayed in touch. I think we both had a hunch my days working for Panic were numbered. We understood that one day, like Ted, I would be forced to leave. We also both knew, from past experience, that we could work effectively together. Given the opportunity, we could be successful pooling our knowledge, our skills, and our passion for building something brand new. After all, we had done precisely that, off and on, for almost two decades.

So, with the advantages I had obtained with my severance package and with Ted already making sales contacts under the name of Pharmascience, I bought in on 1 June 1983.

One thing Ted and I had in common was the belief that we were going to succeed. Our aspirations were not that great. We both agreed that primarily what we wanted from our new business was to make a living and enjoy our careers. In fact, both Ted and I were careful to take the same level of salaries for ourselves that we would pay others. We were both very conservative in our approach to business and never took any bank loans. This must have been one of the aftereffects of growing up during the Great Depression, seeing the devastating effects struggling to pay their bills had on so many people. Many people ended up at the mercy of banks when they could not service their loans.

Ted also believed in following the KISS method of doing business: Keep It Simple, Stupid. We were also prepared to make sacrifices. That first year of Pharmascience, neither Ted nor I drew a salary. But we were operational immediately – Pharmascience hit the ground running.

It was at this point, though, that Ted and I had another decision to make. How were we going to grow our new company? We could proceed the way I had with Winley-Morris some three decades earlier, which meant slowly, step by step. Back then, I had no desire to go public. I had imagined Winley-Morris as a family business and I did not want to cede any control of my company to outside shareholders.

But the situation was markedly different with Pharmascience. For one thing, we were being approached by people who were keen to invest in our new company. This had never been the case with Winley-Morris. In fact, it was not long before I received a call from Sam Grossman, a Montreal accountant I was acquainted with. Sam said he had heard Ted and I might be seeking investors. He added that he had some interesting people in mind, Israelis looking to be part of a Canadian company.

I was not about to become involved with people I did not know, even with a reference from Sam. I have always wanted to size people up before I go into business with them, meet them face-to-face, look them in the eye, and assess their character. I have always insisted on seeing anyone I am dealing with firsthand. With that in mind, I flew to Israel to introduce myself to my prospective investors. Once there, I met Jonathan Zuhovitsky, Shaul Eisenberg's son-in-law. On behalf of the Eisenberg group, Jonathan agreed to invest $200,000 – or what would be twenty percent of our new company's capital – in the fledgling Pharmascience. Shortly after that, I was contacted by Ruby Zimmerman, a fellow Montrealer and owner of the aluminum siding company Zimcor. He asked if he could purchase twenty percent of Eisenberg's investment, mainly, as he confided to me at the time, to try to get close to the elusive Israeli businessman.

While I did not have the chance to deal directly with Eisenberg in Israel, I had heard stories about him. There were certainly lots of them. He was a legendary financier, who was also rumoured, on occasion, to be an Israeli spy, a weapons smuggler, and "the richest Jew in the world." Born in Austria, he had been one of a number of Austrian Jews who fled the Nazis during the Second World War and found safe harbour in a rather unlikely destination – the Japanese-occupied but otherwise free port of Shanghai. Eisenberg's route to safety, east to Siberia and then south through Mongolia, was the stuff of legends. Even so, it all might have been for naught if entreaties from Berlin to expel the Jewish refugees in Shanghai – an estimated 35,000 – had been heeded. Instead, the Japanese refused to do the bidding of their Axis allies. Eisenberg remained in China, where there was some precedent for foreign Jews making a mark. Sun Yat-Sen, the man referred to in China as the "Father of the Nation," the consolidator of that giant country, had a bodyguard and top aide who was Jewish. Morris "Two-Gun" Cohen was a colourful character who, after Sun Yat-Sen's death, reputedly encouraged the Chinese government to abstain from vetoing the 1947 UN resolution to create the Jewish state of Israel.

Anti-Semitism, so prevalent and virulent in Europe in the beginning of the twentieth century, never took hold in Asia, certainly not among the Chinese or the Japanese. All of this goes some way toward explaining Eisenberg's life-long and extremely close ties with China and Chinese officialdom.

Eisenberg eventually moved from Shanghai to Japan, where he married a Japanese woman. From there, he and his family moved to Israel. Eisenberg's influence on Israel had begun even before he immigrated to the country, when he was still living in Japan. The story goes that the Israeli finance minister, Pinchas Sapir, came to Japan to obtain financing to extend the rail lines from Tel Aviv to Be'er Sheba. Sapir had heard about a mysterious trader who could get five percent on loans. All Sapir knew was that this trader was Jewish and his name was Eisenberg. Sapir asked to meet with Eisenberg, hoping to convince him to move his family and all his business to Israel. Eisenberg agreed, on one condition. He wanted the same deal with Israel that he had with Japan, where taxation laws meant that companies did not pay tax on any income made outside the country. Sapir took this under consideration and returned to Israel to pass the law that would from then on be called the "Eisenberg Law." It gave any foreigner who moved to Israel a ten-year tax-free holiday on everything earned outside the country and had a significant impact in attracting more and more foreign capital to Israeli industries. The law lasted for many years and turned out to be one of Eisenberg's significant contributions to the growth of the young nation. Eisenberg was also a trailblazer in opening up trade between Israel and China. And he did so at a time when no Western nation was interested in doing business with China.

He was a wheeler-dealer, a go-between who had connections with the rich and powerful all the over the world. Still, when the Israeli stock market collapsed in the fall of 1983 – rumour has it that he lost $100 million – he returned home from China to discover he had acquired investments he did not want. Pharmascience was one of these. Of course, I had no way of knowing any of this when I was asked by my friend Eric Flanders, Eisenberg's Canadian representative, to attend a meeting with Eisenberg at New York's renowned Waldorf Astoria Hotel. Obviously, I agreed. I didn't see this as anything out of the ordinary. He was my partner, after all.

Or so I thought. Actually, he was about to become my ex-partner. We met and he acknowledged that he had no problem with how I was running my business. He recognized, even in the few months we had been in business together, that Pharmascience was set up to be successful. He could see for himself that we were running a profitable company. Still, I had the feeling that there was a "but" coming and there was. My meeting with this larger-than-life figure could not have lasted more than fifteen minutes; even so I got the clear impression that here was a man who did not waste any time staring at his navel. He made a decision and stuck to it. Eisenberg said, "Mr. Goodman,

I have no business being in your business. I'm a five-per-center. What people would call a middleman. You want to meet the King of Siam, I'm your man. And, by the way, I only deal in cash."

I was surprised by this turn of events, though not particularly upset. I told him there was no problem: I would give him his money back. Then he looked at me and said, "Why don't you come with me to China? I have about forty people working there right now. Mr. Goodman, I will make you a multi-millionaire."

My immediate response was thanks but no thanks. I told him I was happy doing what I was doing. I have no doubt he was serious. In fact, I was flattered that such a man saw something in me that made him want me as part of his high-powered team. But I have no regrets about declining his offer. What was I going to do? Uproot my family? Move to China? That would have been crazy. Roz and I had both decided a decade or so earlier that California would be too much of a culture shock. In any case, I had the sense that anyone working for Eisenberg would always have to answer to Eisenberg. His and only his say would be final. Over the next decade, Eisenberg remained a behind-the-scenes mover and shaker. A testament to his importance in this role is the special visit made by the mayor of Shanghai, an enormously powerful man, to Eisenberg's home in Israel. Eisenberg died of a heart attack in 1997, at the age of seventy-six, on one of his many visits to China.

As for Pharmascience, losing Eisenberg right out of the gate, in our first year, 1983, was another blessing in disguise. It proved to Ted and me that we did not need any outside investor. Once again, I came to the realization that Pharmascience should remain a family business, which it is to this day. I decided I was fine with my new company growing slowly in much the same way that Winley-Morris had grown. That was the model I knew and the one I was most comfortable with. By the way, this business model proved to be too slow for Ruby Zimmerman of Zimcor. He had maintained his investment in Pharmascience, even after Eisenberg withdrew his. But by the late 1980s, Zimmerman was becoming impatient; he was looking to see dividends and we were not paying them. We were reinvesting all of our profits. It took all of ten minutes to buy Ruby Zimmerman out and we parted on friendly terms. He would admit later that he had acted hastily. He had lacked the vision to see what Pharmascience could become. Sometimes, we fail to see the forest for the trees.

Ted and I were also fine with keeping things simple – KISS, remember? — for the time being. We rented a modest, 1,000 square foot space at 839 McCaffrey Street, a small industrial block on the edge of suburban Saint-Laurent. Pharmascience was not housed in the most impressive facilities, but Ted and I were happy to have a place to go and I am sure Ted's wife and their nosy neighbours were glad to have him out of the house. We began by allotting a small space for offices for me, Ted, and our secretaries from ICN – Betty Speevak and Sabina Gabriel respectively. Nowadays, secretaries are called administrative assistants – that is the politically correct term anyway – but whatever they are called I know most senior managers and entrepreneurs could not function without them. I was no exception. Administrative assistants do a lot of things for you that you take for granted. They can, when they are efficient, reduce your workload and allow you to get much more accomplished in a day. Betty worked with me for some three decades, retiring at the age of eighty-two.

Competence was a given for women like Betty Speevak and Sabina Gabriel, Ted Wise's long-time administrative assistant. But it was their remarkable loyalty that never failed to amaze me. For instance, I remember the time at Pharmascience when one of our competitors in Toronto tried to find out from Sabina what we were about to quote on an upcoming hospital tender, vital information that could obviously be used to undercut our bid. Our competitor's plan was to contact Sabina, using a salesman who had previously been employed by ICN Canada. The salesman told her that he wanted her to pass along inside information about our quote on the tender, which would have been corporate espionage. Sabina immediately came to me to tell me what had happened and I told her that it was illegal. Of course, she already knew that. We asked her if she would cooperate with the police in taping this former salesman. She wore a wire, met him in the parking lot, and then passed him the papers. That is when the police stepped in and arrested him. While he got off with a suspended sentence, Sabina had, as usual, demonstrated her capacity for both loyalty and gutsiness.

Our first specialty products at Pharmascience were called Rhinaris Nasal Gel, Rhinaris Nasal Mist, and Secaris. These products came about after I had read a report from Dr. Sheldon Spector. He had completed a study at Hadassah Medical Center in Jerusalem that showed that in ninety percent of cases the vehicle in the steroid preparation was as effective as the steroid preparation itself. I asked myself why a doctor would prescribe a steroid, which has possible side effects, when the vehicle was just as effective and had no side effects. We developed the required formulations for the vehicles alone and marketed them under the trademarked names Rhinaris – for runny noses – and Secaris – for dry, crusty noses.

Meanwhile, Pharmascience's new offices accounted for thirty percent of our total space on McCaffrey with the other seventy percent set aside for our warehouse. Our empty warehouse, I should add. Even the vitamins we were selling were not housed there; they were being shipped from our manufacturer. What Ted and I did have in abundance was well-honed instincts for the vagaries of the pharmaceutical business. In March 1984, less than a year after we began Pharmascience, we learned that the Boston office of the Geneva-based company Serono Laboratories was on the lookout for a new distribution arrangement in Canada. Serono was already the established leader in the soon-to-be burgeoning field of IVF or in-vitro fertilization. Their main product, used to stimulate fertility, was Pergonal, a substance extracted from the urine of postmenopausal women. This urine contains the hormones FSH-LH or Follicular Stimulating Hormone-Luteinizing Hormone. A rather odd fact about Pergonal was that Serono had found that the best place to collect this urine was from Italian nuns. The nunnery provided a large concentration of older women in one place and that made acquiring the necessary quantities of urine much easier.

In this country, the distribution of Pergonal was being handled by Cutter Laboratories, a multinational company whose Canadian headquarters were in Calgary. Based on the information Ted and I had acquired about Serono's desire to change their situation, I made a phone call to Serono's U.S. president, Tom Wiggins, in Boston. I told him I would like to come and talk to him in person.

Conventional wisdom says that cold calls do not work. But that has not been my experience, not if you keep in mind that the idea is to warm up a cold call. Be enthusiastic. Be excited. That approach certainly seemed to work when I phoned Tom Wiggins. In a way, it worked too well. When I offered to come to Boston to meet with Wiggins, he said there was no need for that – he was already planning to come to Canada and he was keen to drop in on us in Montreal and discuss the possibility of having Pharmascience represent him in Canada. This was not the way these transactions were supposed to work. Usually, you went to the prospective customer to try to con-

vince them to do business with you. But Wiggins had invited himself
into our plainly unimpressive headquarters on McCaffrey Street,
which would not provide the first impression we hoped to make. But
how could we prevent him from visiting? I could hardly tell him over
the phone that we did not want him to visit us in Montreal. I still remember the day Wiggins showed up, glanced around at our sparse
offices and even sparser warehouse, and said to me, "What do you
guys do for a living?"

Honesty is the best policy, the saying goes; then again, it is sometimes the only available one. I told my visitor the truth. "Mr. Wiggins," I said. "I have nothing to show you. We are a start-up.
We have been in business less than year." I proceeded to bring him
up to date on my preceding years at ICN and Winley-Morris before
that. I think I may have even told him about my years at the Faculty
of Pharmacy at the University of Montreal. But then I said: "I know
a person, Mr. Wiggins, who has your interest at heart, a person who
also knows me. I would like you to call this fellow for a reference.
And if he tells you that whatever Morris tells you is so, I would like
you to agree to give us the Canadian distribution rights for your
products."

"Who is this person?" Wiggins asked.

"I can't tell you, until you promise. I know we can do a great job
with your product line."

What was I thinking? I have no clue. The offer just came out of
my mouth. I guess I was ad-libbing, tap dancing as fast as I could. I
knew we could not be making the best impression on Wiggins with
what we had on site. So I blurted out this offer, this long-shot bet.
And Wiggins, astonishingly, thought it over for what felt like a very
long time and finally agreed. In retrospect, I think I know why my
unusual strategy worked. If I had told Wiggins who this mysterious
person was right then and there, he would have had no obligation to
do business with me no matter how glowing the reference I received.
I needed him to commit and he had. More important, he was in-
trigued by the offer and by my, well, what else could you call it, my
chutzpah. This successful negotiation had very little to do, I realize
now, with any business acumen I had acquired over the years. What
I was relying on instead was my knowledge of human nature. His curiosity was piqued. Of course, I was not asking him to put any of this
in writing. I was willing to trust his word.

My mystery man was Hans Thierstein, Serono's own chief financial officer in Geneva. I had worked with Hans at ICN, where he was vice-president of finance, for almost twelve years and he could vouch for both Ted and me. I was absolutely sure he would give us a glowing recommendation. He must have, because two weeks later Wiggins called to say, "We're giving Pharmascience a three-year contract." Business is not always, as most people think, about winners and losers, but in this case it was. After Wiggins agreed to transfer his business to Pharmascience, I knew he would have the distasteful task of letting Cutter, the former Canadian distributor for Serono, know about this change in arrangements. To his credit, Wiggins flew out to Calgary to break the bad news in person.

None of this directly involved Pharmascience or me, at least not until I received a call from Calgary. Wiggins was dealing with Cutter's extremely upset general manager, who was understandably angry about losing Serono, a company that Cutter had been in business with for fifteen years. Mainly, he felt it was unfair that he was getting a termination notice of only thirty days. Serono's contract with Cutter allowed for just such an abrupt parting of the ways, but Cutter's GM appealed to Wiggins on another basis. This loss would hit him hard, personally. He would be unable to reach his planned budgeted sales goal and he would lose his bonus.

I must have surprised Wiggins when I told him I agreed with the distraught GM in Calgary. I also thought the abrupt nature of the termination was unfair. After all, I knew that I would feel the same way if I were in this man's shoes. So I offered an unusual compromise, based on the fact, as I told Wiggins, that it was Pharmascience's intention to be in business with Serono for a long time. In any case, I suggested we would turn over to Cutter every penny we earned on the Serono account from the first day we took over in March until Cutter's year-end at the end of October. "You'll do that?" Wiggins asked, stunned by my generous and unsolicited offer. I told him I would for one reason – it was the right thing to do. The Golden Rule is not taught in business schools, but this was an example that proves it might not be such a bad idea if it were.

Pharmascience ended up representing Serono for the next six years and over that time the company's sales of Serono's products increased from $250,000 in 1984 to $10 million in 1990. This business accounted for sixty percent of Pharmascience's gross profits in 1990.

But by 1990 Serono had grown in its stature as the world-wide leader in the booming specialty IVF industry – IVF was in its infancy, so to speak, when we took over Canadian distribution for Serono – and the company felt it had to establish its own marketing and sales team in Canada. However, Serono was prepared to make us an un-usual and surprisingly generous offer. Serono recalled our sympa-thetic gesture when we took over from Cutter, and they repaid us with a similar gesture on an even grander scale, demonstrating some-thing rare in large corporations, an institutional memory. They re-membered what we had done to help them out of a difficult situation with Cutter and they were grateful. What Serono was offering Phar-mascience was a kind of buy-out bonus. It has to be emphasized they had no contractual obligation to do this. Nevertheless, they decided to compensate Pharmascience with twenty-five percent of Serono's Canadian sales for the next three years. All we had to do was handle the shipping on their behalf. In plain terms, this meant we were going to receive two million dollars a year for three years for doing a min-imal amount of work. What gratifies me most about this turn of events is that it came from behaving like a mensch and being recog-nized for doing so with great generosity. This is a rare occurrence in the corporate world. I should also add that we have never tried to make a generic of any of Serono's products.

As of June 1990, Pharmascience would lose Serono, its biggest client – our sales were about to drop by fifty percent – but Ted and I also had an unexpected opportunity to take what was basically found money, our buyout, and invest it. Which we did. The entire six mil-lion dollars went into research and development. In the long run, that would make all the difference in how quickly and how big Pharma-science would grow over the next two decades.

There is another part to the story of our relationship with Tom Wig-gins. When Tom left Serono, he founded a bio-tech company called Connetics, in Palo Alto, California. His new company was doing re-search on a drug called Relaxin, which was to be used in the treatment of scleroderma, a devastating skin condition that had no effective treat-ment at the time. By that time my son Jonathan was working at Phar-mascience and Tom called him to see whether we would be interested in investing in a Phase III study. (Moving to Phase III meant he had al-ready gotten positive results in a Phase II study.) Jonathan felt indebted to Tom and through Paladin, the company Jonathan had started in July 1995, invested several million dollars, mainly out of gratitude to

Tom. Unfortunately, the study failed. There is still no treatment for scleroderma; Connetics eventually sold all world rights for Relaxin to Novartis. The only exception was the Canadian rights, which are still held by Paladin. Relaxin is currently in clinical trials for the treatment of acute heart failure. Should this drug prove effective, Paladin will have the rights to the research currently being paid for by Novartis and Jonathan believes that its value in treating this condition may be worth more than the current value of Paladin as a whole. Once again, better to be lucky than smart.

10

Swinging for the Fences

Life is either a daring adventure, or nothing.
Helen Keller

A career progresses in unpredictable ways. There is hard work, obviously, and vision, and there is also serendipity. That cold call I made to Serono, for instance, could hardly have occurred at a better time as far as Pharmascience's early success was concerned. Similarly, the way in which Pharmascience parted company with Serono could not have happened in a more advantageous way as far as our company's enduring future was concerned.

I suppose it comes down to this: from the time I was a delivery boy for Manny Winrow, I have always believed in one philosophy of business, which, as it turns out, is the same as my philosophy of living: keep moving forward and, perhaps just as important, keep looking forward. The "vision thing" is what I have heard this momentum called in the last few decades. It can also be described as a positive outlook, part of my nature, I am sure. My experience has also shown that success breeds success. Certainly my early years building Pharmascience provided plenty of opportunities to go from strength to strength, to build one small success upon another.

It has also helped that I am, by nature, a deeply curious person. My son David has referred to this trait of mine as "my non-arrogance." He can tell you that I walk into any space with the intention of learning something new. "My father doesn't have a lot of attitude," as David has put it. "He's always eager to work, eager to know more. I think that's why he is still very excited about going to work every day. He just keeps on learning." Roz, too, can attest to all the hours

I have spent poring over medical journals, always on the lookout for new ideas, new uses for drugs, for some unique treatment that will alleviate the suffering of patients.

This also explains how my curiosity led me, in 1987, to become increasingly fascinated with a ground-breaking article I stumbled across in the prestigious *New England Journal of Medicine*. It was written by a doctor in California, William Summers. Summers was conducting studies employing a pre-existing drug, Tacrine Hydrochloride, to treat patients with a neurological disorder that was, at the time, often misdiagnosed as dementia or senility. Tacrine Hydrochloride had originally been used during the First World War as an antidote to mustard gas, a battlefield poison designed to destroy a soldier's nervous system. Mustard gas was a gruesome development in the use of chemicals in warfare and Tacrine had some early success combating it, at least if the circumstances were right. Unfortunately, that "if" was a big one, especially in the midst of battle. What Summers discovered, some seventy years later, was that Tacrine belonged to a class of drugs called cholinesterase inhibitors and that it might, as such, be able to reduce the symptoms of patients suffering with Alzheimer's Disease.

This manner of research is not particularly uncommon – an older drug once used for a particular disease or disorder is found, years later, sometimes with a good deal of success, not to mention very little expenditure, to be useful in treating a different disorder or disease. This is similar to my experience with Ribavirin, Milan Panic's purported cure for the common cold, which came back as an effective treatment for hepatitis C and seems now to be showing enormous promise as a cancer treatment.

However, when it came to Tacrine Hydrochloride, it is hard to deny how remarkable the story of this drug is. Think about it: here was a drug that had been around since 1918, ignored for decades (thankfully there have been no mustard gas attacks in recent years), suddenly rediscovered and showing the potential to treat the devastating symptoms of an increasingly terrifying disease.

To be honest, I did not know much about Alzheimer's back then. Not many people did. This seems hard to believe today, but Alzheimer's was not in the news or in the public consciousness the way it is now. What is referred to as early-onset Alzheimer's was rarely diagnosed at the time. Also, as I suggested earlier, medical thinking about the disorder was often confused with the thinking about senility. All I really knew was that Alzheimer's was a neurolog-ical disorder. Nevertheless, this knowledge was enough to spark my intense interest. After all, in the early 1970s, first at Winley-Morris and then at ICN Canada, I had been fascinated by the successes achieved by the drug L-DOPA in treating Parkinson's, another myste-rious and devastating neurological disorder.

Reading Dr. William Summers's article on Tacrine Hydrochloride in the *New England Journal of Medicine*, I felt much the same way as I had when I first became involved with L-DOPA; I was extremely excited. I still remember saying to Roz that I could not understand how I had never heard of this drug before. I began my own research, intent on satisfying my own curiosity. I immediately looked Tacrine up in my old textbooks and discovered that a company in Melbourne, Australia, was manufacturing it in combination with morphine and marketing it as a painkiller.

Incidentally, this is the fun stuff for me. It is a lot like being a de-tective. You come across a study, a particular drug that could change countless lives, and then you employ all your skills, your creativity and resources, to seeking it out. Then, eventually, you find yourself in the position of manufacturing and distributing it. Frankly, this is thrilling. It is precisely the kind of thrill that has kept me passionate about this business for more than sixty years.

What is more, Tacrine had the potential of being a breakthrough drug; I sensed that from the start. In the pharmaceutical business, you should always be trying to hit the homerun that will change the mar-ketplace and, even more important, the quality of people's lives. But the truth is that homeruns are rare and, while I am not much of a baseball fan or even a sports fan for that matter, I do relate to the idea of swinging for the fences, to borrow a sports term. In musical terms, something I am more familiar with, it is like listening to a great tenor reaching for the high note. Simply put, you take a big risk in order to land a big reward. It is what this business, at its most satis-fying, is all about.

This kind of thinking explains why Roz and I booked a flight bound for Melbourne as soon as I could arrange it. As far as I was concern-ed, there was no time to lose. The first part of my plan was straight-forward: nail down the supply of Tacrine for the Canadian market.

I did make one important stop on the way to Melbourne. I stopped in California to visit Dr. William Summers. I wanted to make contact with him personally. It is one thing to read an article; it is another to meet the person who has devoted himself to the research, the clinical work, and everything else that went into writing that article. The person who knows his subject inside-out and is totally committed to it. That describes William Summers. When I met him, he already knew more about Tacrine than anyone else in the world. He was also a fascinating character. In my experience, Summers was the kind of professional you so often find doing this sort of challenging and frequently ground-breaking research. One thing was apparent from the start – he was not doing any of this for the money. Instead, he was dedicated to fighting Alzheimer's; that was what drove him. That and pure scientific curiosity. His dedication, and the dedication of all those who do this kind of research, always strikes me as remarkable. These are special people, rare people, and it is a fact I have always made sure to remember.

My experience in Australia was a study in contrasts. The word dedication was not the one that immediately came to mind when I finally arrived in Melbourne and met with the owner of the company that was selling Tacrine, combined with morphine, as a painkiller. Here was a man who could hardly have cared less about the pharmaceutical business. As it turned out, he had inherited the company from an uncle. He was really in the toy business. Between that and the yachts he enjoyed spending his time on, Tacrine did not hold any special interest for him. He did not see its potential. He had never even heard of Alzheimer's. Our negotiations were remarkably quick and easy. I came home with five kilos of Tacrine, manufactured in Australia. More important, I had acquired the technical know-how to manufacture the drug – all of this for $50,000.

I returned to Montreal itching to get started on this new project. The next part of my plan began with my realization that I needed to meet Dr. Serge Gauthier. He was at McGill, in charge of geriatric medicine, a field that obviously included Alzheimer's. So I went to the Montreal Neurological Institute in December 1988 with the intention of tracking him down. The search did not require me to be much of a detective. As I arrived in the entranceway of the Neurological Institute, I asked the first distinguished-looking gentleman I met where I might find Dr. Gauthier. He laughed and replied that I had found him. We both seemed to sense that this impromptu meeting was going to be important for both of us.

"I have a product I think will be of interest to you: Tacrine Hydrochloride," I said.

"And so, tell me, are you my Santa Claus?" he replied.

"Maybe," I said.

"Well, I'm very, very interested. I want to do a clinical trial with Tacrine."

"I don't have the money for clinical research," I explained, but I added that I could provide him with the drug for his study, free of charge. In that case, he said he would be able to arrange for the funding. A deal was made on the spot.

Dr. Gauthier had read the same Summers article I had in the *New England Journal of Medicine*. Every neurologist who was paying attention had. It had all the earmarks of being a breakthrough article. But Dr. Gauthier, excited as he was by this new research, had no way of getting his hands on Tacrine – at least, not until I showed up out of the blue, offering to provide him with an unlimited supply of the drug, free of charge. So, yes, I understand how even a Jewish boy named Goodman, with no beard or belly to speak of, must have looked a lot like Santa Claus to Dr. Gauthier on that particular day. Here, again, is an example of how good timing comes into the picture. Around the same time Dr. Gauthier and his wife, Louise – an occupational therapist – were teaming up to begin a multi-centre Canadian study on Tacrine, I was paid a visit by Harry Stratford. Stratford was head of the small English company Shire Pharmaceuticals. Shire was no more than a few years old then and when Stratford first came to see me, his purpose was to interest Pharmascience in the research his company was doing on hormonal therapy for women. He very much wanted to develop a generic version of Premarin. But during his meeting with Ted Wise and me, we recognized an opportunity to tell Stratford about Tacrine. Stratford flew home to England, did his own research on the drug, and the next thing we knew he was back in Montreal negotiating for exclusive development rights with Pharmascience.

"Mr. Goodman, you can give this drug to any multinational in England and they'll grab it, but I want it and I can promise you I'll do something with it," Stratford said. His proposal was convincing. It also struck a chord with me, probably because it was pretty much the same proposal I had made to Tom Wiggins at Serono.

I had also heard lots of stories about multinationals burying important research because they had other interests. Not to mention cases where important research had been shelved because the research would end up being in conflict with another product the company was developing. Sometimes, these decisions were made for financial reasons; sometimes a big company would just lose track of a promising drug or put it on the back burner because something more important or more profitable had come along.

So I leveled with Stratford. "I'm afraid of working with multi-nationals because I'm afraid they'll take Tacrine and put it aside and not develop it. I want to work with someone who will develop it."

To his credit, Stratford proved to be that person. We signed our initial agreement with his company in November 1988. Stratford arranged for financing with Schroder Ventures for a multi-centre study in England. This involved a group of very influential neurologists throughout England. Their studies would eventually endorse the use of Tacrine.

What I did not know at the time and would read about later in a book called *Flying High*, a chronicle of Shire Pharmaceutical's first twenty years, is how significant this meeting was for Harry Stratford. Shire has become a huge multinational. Its sales exceed two billion dollars and the company employs close to 3,000 people. When I first met Harry Stratford, though, things were not going quite so well. The company's situation is accurately described in *Flying High*: "Stratford and his company had been floundering financially. He and his wife, Carole, conceded that their credit cards had been 'maxed out.' But Tacrine opened the door for the struggling Shire company."

I was wrong, though, when I told Harry Stratford at our first meeting that I thought multinationals would not proceed with the R&D on Tacrine. A year after my negotiations with Stratford and Shire, the giant multinational Warner-Lambert was developing Tacrine in the United States. I immediately felt pressured to move fast, to try to beat out the competition in Canada. So I wrote to every Canadian neurologist interested in doing clinical research, offering them the capsules for free. Within twenty-four hours, I received an enthusiastic response. There was just one problem: the phone call came from a doctor in the United States.

Bonnie Davis was on staff at the Mount Sinai Hospital in New York City and she was calling to request one hundred capsules for her research program, capsules I was not in a position to send her. Pharmascience could not send drugs across the border unless they had been cleared by the Federal Drug Administration (FDA) and

Tacrine still wasn't. In fact, I said to her straight out, "Dr. Davis, don't you know you have an FDA?"

Still, I was curious to know how she knew about my offer to the neurologists across the border from her. "We have friends," she said evasively. "What do you mean you have friends?" I persisted, adding that I had not sent any notices about Tacrine to the United States. Her "friends" she finally explained were at McMaster University in Hamilton. "They told us about you," she said. "They told me to call you." She also made it clear that her patient, whose identity she would not reveal, was a very important person.

Her connection with McMaster gave me an idea. I suggested she send her patient to McMaster, at which point Pharmascience would be both permitted and happy to supply her patient with capsules. Dr. Davis did not seem interested in this plan and our conversation ended. I assumed I had heard the end of all this intrigue. But ten minutes later the telephone rang again. The call was from a Dr. Michael Davidson, who was coincidentally calling from Mount Sinai, too, and, even more coincidentally, requesting Tacrine capsules. Incidentally, Dr. Davidson spoke with an accent that was very familiar to me.

"Are you Israeli?" I guessed. He said he was. At which point I informed him, as I had just informed Bonnie Davis, that if his patient was in the U.S., I could not help him. I had an idea, though. I said if his patient was in Israel then there would be no problem. "The patient is in Israel," he said quickly, perhaps a little too quickly. Still, I agreed to provide the capsules to an Israeli company that could see to his request. In fact, Davidson and I had an acquaintance in common at that company – the chairman of Teva, Eli Hurwitz. It also turned out I had had dinner with Eli in Tel Aviv two weeks earlier. I suggested Dr. Davidson call this mutual acquaintance, but I did not expect him to do it right away. After all, it was 3 a.m., Israeli time. But Davidson called, waking up Eli, who then called me and said he would take care of the matter. He said I should send him the capsules, so I did.

From the start, there was a deliberate logic to my suggesting Israel rather than the United States as the best place to treat Dr. Davidson's patient. I knew that if the case ever ended up going to court in Israel the Jewish law of *Pikuach Nefesh* – the saving of a soul – would inevitably come into effect. This law, which I should add that I am enormously proud of as a Jew, essentially states that matters of life and death always take precedence over everything else. So even before Teva agreed to take responsibility for Tacrine, this was what was in my mind when I agreed to send the drug to Israel.

Once the drug and Davidson's patient were both in Israel, I assumed, incorrectly once again, that I had heard the last of all this. But a few weeks later, a very excited Bonnie Davis called and before she even said hello, she said, "It works. The drug works!" This was puzzling since, as far as I knew, I had never sent her the drug. I still had not quite put together the connection between Dr. Davidson and Dr. Davis. I said as much to Bonnie and she explained. The patient in Israel was, in fact, her patient.

"We flew him from the U.S. to Israel with a nurse," she went on. "We put him up in the Hilton Hotel in Tel Aviv and we treated him in his hotel room. The patient is now able to tie a knot in his tie! I don't know if you understand what that means for an Alzheimer's patient. But it is big, big progress!"

On 14 February 1989, on a flight with Roz, travelling from Los Angeles to Phoenix, I was reading the editorial page in the prestigious *Wall Street Journal* and came across the story of a patient named Roy Gabbard who was being treated with a drug called THA that had somehow been obtained from a company in Montreal that was "currently supplying the drug to Alzheimer's researchers in Canada and Europe." The company was Pharmascience. The drug, THA, was Tacrine Hydrochloride. I don't know how he procured it; we never sold Tacrine to the U.S., but I was stunned and overjoyed nonetheless. I remember looking over at Roz and saying, "You won't believe what I'm reading. You won't believe it. Pharmascience is mentioned in the editorial of the *Wall Street Journal*."

The article went a long way toward putting our still small company on the map; it also created considerable controversy because, as I mentioned, THA was not authorized for sale in the United States. However, spurred on by the *Wall Street Journal* article and the Alzheimer's Society of America, the FDA had to answer for the fact that they were dragging their feet on authorizing the drug that was helping to slow symptoms in people with an incurable disease. People like Roy Gabbard.

Not so coincidentally, this was when the FDA reached the conclusion that the worrisome side effect that was showing up in clinical studies of Tacrine – namely liver toxicity – was manageable, something we all already knew. Whatever the FDA's reasons for changing their mind about Tacrine, they were finally doing the right thing. They were giving people hope. Still, they informed Warner-Lambert that one more clinical study was required, after which the drug would be cleared to go on the market. The FDA, it seemed, had also recognized the priority of saving a single life as laid out in Jewish law. Or it was at least finally willing to accept that the risks of the drug could be managed and that there was value in providing Alzheimer's patients and their families with some measure of hope where no hope existed before. And Tacrine does, for a period of time at least, offer some relief from the more devastating symptoms of Alzheimer's.

Warner-Lambert was aware of the multi-centre study being conducted by Shire in England. They contacted Harry Stratford and asked to buy the clinical studies Shire had been conducting in England, which would give Warner-Lambert the second study they needed. At this point, Pharmascience accepted Shire's offer of $1.5 million for the rights to sell the clinical study.

Given that Pharmascience had a contract with Shire that gave us control over the studies they were paying for, why did I agree to let Shire sell their research? First, I had not put a significant amount of money into researching the drug at the time Shire wanted to purchase it. I suppose I could have blocked Shire, but, other than asking for more money, I did not see the point in holding things up. Most of all, I wanted to see the drug succeed. I wanted to see it help people suffering with Alzheimer's.

After that phone call out of the blue from Bonnie Davis, my relationship with her continued and progressed. A few years later, I also assisted her with another medication intended to treat dementia, Galantamine Hydrochloride, which I helped her obtain a patent for. In fact, my name appears on one of her patents. Later, she sold the drug to Shire Laboratories, bringing the whole story full circle. Eventually, Galantamine became a worldwide product licensed to Janssen Pharmaceuticals and sold under the trade name Reminyl. In December 2012, Pharmascience received authorization from Health Canada to sell the generic version of Galantamine.

Tacrine never would be cleared for sale in Canada. As the complicated story of this drug demonstrates, regulatory boards, like the FDA in the United States and Health Canada here, have become, sometimes for better, sometimes for worse, an integral part of the pharmaceutical industry. In the case of Serge Gauthier's clinical research on

Tacrine, Health Canada's Dr. Cathy Petersen was never convinced that the rewards that might be gained from the drug outweighed the risks, especially the risks associated with the possibility of increases in liver enzymes. And, in the end, Cathy Petersen had the final say in this matter, as in all others.

Our relationship with Health Canada and Cathy Petersen, in particular, has always been an open one. I have always respected her decisions and their integrity, even when I did not always like what she was telling me, which was the case with Tacrine. I remember after she definitively decided that Tacrine would not go on the market, I asked her what would happen when Warner-Lambert came calling with their lobbyists and started pressuring Health Canada to have the drug cleared. After all, they would want to market the drug all over the world, including Canada, especially after obtaining approval from the FDA.

"Morris," Cathy said. "You don't have to worry about that. Whatever I tell you I will tell everybody." She was true to her word. Cathy has also been forthright in our personal relationship. I am still touched by her response to a call I made to her some twenty years ago now. It was shortly after my son Jonathan had been diagnosed with Hodgkins Disease. I told her, "Dr. Petersen, I have a personal problem. I need advice about my son's treatment."

She was immediately sympathetic and reassuring. She told me her daughter's husband had Hodgkins and he was okay. She said that I should not worry too much and that she would have somebody call me with more information. It took about three minutes from the moment I got off the phone with Cathy until the head of Toronto's Princess Margaret Hospital, one of the best cancer research hospitals in the country, called. Cathy had given her my number. The administrator said if I needed anything I should call. I never did, but I will always remember the compassion Cathy showed me at that difficult time.

Pharmascience has also won some arguments with Cathy over the years. For instance, when, around 2000, we came out with Methadone as a treatment in palliative care, Cathy said we had to prove the drug's efficacy before Health Canada could clear it. I told her that no one was going to do the studies needed to show that because, since there were no patents for it, there would be no profit. However there was a need for it. My argument was that there were similar drugs on the market in England and the United States, so why shouldn't it be available here in Canada? "Can you get me a sample you can compare it to?" Cathy asked. We did and she changed her decision and cleared it.

As for Tacrine, a new drug, Donepezil (marketed under the name Aricept by Pfizer), eventually replaced it in the marketplace. The new drug has the virtue of having fewer side effects and being deemed safer. Unfortunately, the new drug has, like Tacrine, not advanced the fight against Alzheimer's in the way we had originally hoped it would in those early, heady days of research after William Summers's study was published. Or after Dr. Gauthier and Shire's research was done, or after Tacrine was finally cleared everywhere but here. The simple, heartbreaking fact is that, after spending billions of dollars on research over the past twenty years, we still do not know what causes Alzheimer's or how to treat it effectively.

Pharmascience's interest in Alzheimer's has not diminished. We are currently supplying Naproxen tablets, a popular anti-inflammatory drug, and the required placebos, free of charge to Dr. John Breitner at Montreal's Douglas Hospital. Breitner is investigating the idea that if the inflammation in the brain of people suffering with Alzheimer's can be diminished there may be beneficial effects for patients. We will only know the results in years to come.

Morris and Rosalind's wedding in 1961

Manny Winrow at Morris and Rosalind's wedding

Left to right: Milton and May Feier, Rosalind and Morris, Miriam and
Myron Pantzer

Rosalind Goodman's graduation from McGill
(Bachelor of Arts) in 1963

Jules Gilbert

Morris Goodman's concern is building a leading health-care company in Canada

A 1972 *Time* magazine ad from the ICN years

Morris and Ted Wise at a tradeshow in 1985

Team-building at Pharmascience (Morris and Ted Wise), 1980s

Jonathan Goodman, Val Gorbatyuk, and Morris in 1988

Jonathan Goodman, David Goodman, Morris, and Morris's architect nephew, Jerry Covienski

Left to right: Mario Deschamps (president of Pharmascience), Pierre Bourque (mayor of Montreal), Bernard Landry (premier of Quebec), Morris, David Goodman, Jonathan Goodman, and Ted Wise

Dr. Paul Melekhov in 2003

Morris's 75th birthday dinner. Left to right: Jack Kay, Morris, Milan Panic, and Dick Mackay. Seated: Ted Wise

Pharmascience from generation to generation: David and Morris in 2007

Morris and Ted Wise on Pharmascience's 25th anniversary in 2008

George Montgomery on Pharmascience's
25th anniversary in 2008

Morris and Ronald Reuben in 2009

Jonathan and Morris, 2013

Debbie Goodman and Gerry Davis's wedding in 1991

Mia Melmed and David Goodman's wedding in 1995

Dana Caplan and Jonathan Goodman's wedding in 2004

Shawna Goodman and Todd Sone's Wedding in 1996

Morris and Rosalind cruising the world

Traveling the world

White water rafting in Bali

The Goodman family in 2007 (Orly was not yet born)

Debbie Goodman presenting her book *Speeding Down the Spiral*
to Morris and Rosalind

Shawna Goodman-Sone and her book *Panache*

Rosalind receives the Leadership award from Federation CJA. Left to right: Senator Yoine Goldstein, Rosalind, Susan Laxer, and Stanley Plotnick

Morris awarded an honorary doctorate from McGill University. Left to right: Principal Heather Munroe-Blum, Dean of Medicine Richard Levin, Morris, Chancellor Arnold Steinberg, Chair of McGill University Board of Directors Stuart H. "Kip" Cobbett, Director of Goodman Cancer Research Centre Dr. Michel Tremblay)

Rosalind awarded an honorary doctorate from McGill University. From left to right: Principal Heather Munroe-Blum, Dean of Medicine Richard Levin, Rosalind, Chancellor Arnold Steinberg, Chair of McGill University Board of Directors Stuart H. "Kip" Cobbett, and Director of Goodman Cancer Research Centre Dr. Michel Tremblay.

Morris, President of the State of Israel Shimon Peres, and Rosalind in 2012

Rector of the University of Montreal Guy Breton and Morris in 2013

Jean Coutu and Morris share a laugh at the University of Montreal

The Agora at the University of Montreal

The dedication of the Goodman Cancer Research Centre and Bellini Life Sciences Complex. Morris, Rosalind, Dr. Richard Levin, Marisa Bellini, Dr. Martin Grant, Dr. Francesco Bellini, and Principal Heather Munroe-Blum

Rosalind and Morris in front of the Rosalind and Morris Goodman Cancer Research Centre, 2013

Pharmascience Meets the World

Blessed is the son who studies with his father,
and blessed is the father who teaches his son.
The Talmud

By the 1990s, Pharmascience was well on its way to becoming the little company that could, not just in this country but all around the world. Some forty years earlier, when my first company, Winley-Morris, was just getting off the ground and I was flying from coast to coast across Canada, I had experienced, a sense of endless possibility. "All I have to do is want this. That is all I have to do to succeed," I had thought back then, looking down over this country's great expanses. I had a similar feeling at the beginning of the 1990s as Pharmascience began to branch out internationally, making its mark from Great Britain to Israel, from Vietnam to the Ukraine. My thoughts once more were on the future: "It is all there for me ... for everyone." Opportunity seemed endless.

In its start-up years, Pharmascience was a modest operation; there was no way to deny that fact. I still laugh every time I recall Serono president Tom Wiggins's visit to our first under-furnished, under-staffed office on McCaffrey Street and his dismissive remark, "What do you guys do for a living?" Of course, that did not mean my partner Ted Wise and my goals were modest. From the start, our vision for Pharmascience far exceeded our circumstances. In his introductory message to our website, my son David, now CEO of Pharmascience, describes the founding of the company this way:

Their [David is referring to Ted and me] courage would be tested immediately. After all, they had no factory, no staff, no product, no distributors, and very little money. Their only resource lay in their heads, in their hearts, and in their dream. That was all they needed to begin turning their vision into reality.

David has played a big part in shaping that vision and that reality, particularly with regard to Pharmascience's international expansion. Like his sisters and brother, David was used to hanging around my various offices. As a boy, he routinely came into work with me on Sundays. As he grew older, he began working for Pharmascience during his school vacations. For instance, in the summer of 1983, during the very first days of Pharmascience, he worked in our warehouse as an assistant in our shipping department. The following two summers David, who was then in his early twenties, worked as a travelling salesperson, detailing doctors in the old-fashioned way, face-to-face. He sometimes found himself in rather isolated locations in Northern Ontario and Quebec. In effect, he was doing what I had done at around the same age some thirty years earlier at Winley-Morris. It was a unique adventure for a young man, one he still remembers with fondness:

That summer Nordair was still in business. You could fly unlimited for $100 or some ridiculously small amount like that as long as you didn't mind flying standby – sometimes, I confess, I never did get off the ground. In any case, I came up with a plan to buy one of these passes to fly to places like Thunder Bay and Sault Ste. Marie and sometimes I would just go for the day. Either that or I'd drive around the area and then if I got homesick I could fly home for the weekend. The Nordair offer was one of those great deals I'm pretty sure I used more than anyone else. I got to go up to some of the same places my dad had gone when he was a young man. Like James Bay, which probably didn't look very different from the way it looked when my father visited it in the 1950s. I was so much younger than all the other drug reps there that I felt special. I even remember getting approached by someone from Parke-Davis at the time who offered me a job. I don't know if he knew that I was Morris Goodman's son, but I think they just liked the idea of having someone in that rather remote area. For my part, I had no experience as a salesman. I guess Ted Wise gave me a quick lesson, what I would call a "15-minuter" and that was pretty much it. I don't even know how well I knew what we were selling back then, but people were buying. My second summer my father also hired a friend of mine to accompany me. I remember it as a lot of fun.

In 1994, when David officially joined the company, he was twenty-nine. He had a bachelor's degree in commerce and had just earned his PhD in pharmacology from the University of Virginia. The latter was an impressive accomplishment, especially when you consider that he had once been told by a high school guidance counselor that he did not have an aptitude for science. For a while, I believe he accepted this foolish pronouncement and I am guessing that explains his undergraduate degree in commerce. But he did not give up on science. Instead, he worked hard and proved that high school guidance counselor dead wrong. In fact, he was contemplating continuing his education in science and doing a post-doctoral degree when I offered him a job at Pharmascience. My children will tell you that when it comes to their careers I have never tried to push them in one direction or another. I always liked the fact they were interested in a wide variety of things. Or as David puts it:

> My father wasn't the kind of parent who told you what to do or, more important, what to become. In some ways, it was a little hard growing up with him as your father because he would never say this is what you are going to do. That was not his way. He never pushed any of us.

I have always wanted my children to expand their worlds as much as possible. And while my sons, David and Jonathan, have followed in my footsteps, my daughters, Debbie and Shawna, have found success in worlds very different from my own – art and food, respectively. In addition, both my daughters have always involved themselves in philanthropic pursuits. This is hardly surprising, of course, since they are also following in their mother's footsteps.

The strength of David's personality is evident in everything he has done, from being on his high school *Reach for the Top* team – *Reach for the Top* was a popular quiz show for high school students, which was on CBC from 1961 to 1985 – to his career, where he has risen to the top at Pharmascience. As he would probably tell you, his most important and, I believe, most undervalued quality is perseverance. David is a plugger. He has also shown great maturity well beyond his years. He is never anything but honourable. He has always been thoughtful of others.

Still, perhaps because of his methodical approach, David has probably been subject to a little more of a "push" from me when it came to his choice of career than my other children. For instance, by the time David received his PhD in pharmacology, it was clear that he had arrived at a crossroads. If he decided to pursue his academic career, he would have to move from where he was living at the time. He had moved a lot during his twenties and he was feeling the strain of this impending choice. The academic position being offered to him would end in two years; he would come away from it with a post-doctoral degree, but in all likelihood would be uprooted yet again. All of this meant any plans he might have to settle down would be impossible.

I married at twenty-nine, which was considered late then, and I think David, who was the same age when he joined Pharmascience, was also beginning to feel it was time for him to put down roots. If he wanted to start a personal relationship, for instance, he knew that would be much harder to do if he was living what was, in effect, a nomadic academic life. So when he mentioned to me that he was considering doing a post-doctoral degree, I was frank with him. I said, "Is that really what you want to do with your life? What are you going to get out of that in the long run? There is an opportunity for you right here ... at Pharmascience."

I suppose I broke my own rule in this case. I engaged in what David has since called "gentle coercion." But he established himself in the company right from the start. As he puts it, joining Pharmascience was, in the final analysis, "an easy decision to make":

When I came into Pharmascience, my dad said to me, "You'll trail after me." I confess I wondered if I should start in this department or that one, get a feel for the company from a variety of positions – get introduced to the whole big picture. But Dad said, "What do you want to do that for? Just do what I tell you." So I did. The adjustment was easy. I knew what I was getting into. I knew my Dad's style. I was a bit like his secretary at the start. But it wasn't long before he was giving me the chance to make things happen. Also, when I started, Ted Wise, my father's partner, was still at Pharmascience and my dad and Ted split up the responsibilities for the business with Ted focusing on sales and marketing and my father focusing on research and development, business development, new products. That's what he wanted me to step in and handle. I believe he felt the sales and marketing side was well covered. I was meant to concentrate on expanding the vision of the company.

With David's professional life settled, he has found a rich, full personal life. He married Mia Melmed, daughter of Calvin and Carolyn Melmed, on 8 June 1995 at the Shaar Hashomayim Congregation. Mia has a law degree from the University of Ottawa and passed her Quebec bars, making her career working in the field of adoption. She has exceptional organizational skills and has also built a beautiful home for David. She is a wonderful life-mate for him and a devoted mother to their thirteen-year-old daughter, Julia. Julia, a graduate of Akiva Elementary School, now attends Miss Edgar's and Miss Cramp's School.

It has been rewarding for me to work with David at Pharmascience, to watch him voluntarily follow my path. But sometimes I suspect it has been harder for him to work with me than it has been for me to work with him. He has always been respectful of the fact that I always had the last say. Still, David is very much his own man. We have a working relationship in which we do not always see eye-to-eye but we are still able to respect each other's point of view.

From early on, David accepted the challenge of spearheading new ventures like our Pharmascience branch in England, which we called Dominion Pharmacal, reviving the name of my first company after I left ICN. Before David joined Pharmascience, any opportunities we might have had on the international scene were treated in a less organized way. International opportunities were not built into the structure of the company so it was kind of catch-as-catch-can. If we received a fax from a company overseas expressing interest in our products, or interest in having us distribute their products, I would usually assign someone rather junior in the company to take care of it. But that changed with David. David brought structure to the international side of our business.

At the same time, I began to realize that David shares my curiosity, my interest in following a lead that has the potential to make a difference, not necessarily a fortune. Here, again, is David's perspective:

If my father was going to invest his time, he was always more interested in investing in people or in the potential of new products. He has never worried about whether something is going to make money or work one ... two ... three. I meet a lot of people in business who see it as their job to filter out any idea they think might not be successful. They don't give the idea a chance and the instinct to react this way often becomes stronger as they get older. My Dad has very good filters, but he doesn't allow them to prevent him from giving new ideas and, in particular, new people a chance.

This has made it possible for him to find success in places where he didn't expect or plan to find it. That was true of that summer job he gave me. I was his son, of course, but he still gave me a chance to try something different and to prove myself. He also gave me the chance to build my confidence.

In retrospect, it is easy to see that for David these new business ventures in Europe and later Asia followed a similar pattern to the adventures he had had as a young man learning the ropes travelling through Northern Ontario and Northern Quebec. Only now it was on a larger scale. And this time David was not flying standby.

When David started at Pharmascience, he and I travelled together a lot and I offloaded a lot of these new international opportunities onto him. He handled them all with skill and imagination, demonstrating an innate talent for forming personal relationships with the people Pharmascience was doing business with. I think I have played some part in helping him understand just how important personal relationships are in business.

Dominion Pharmacal is a case in point. It was the outgrowth of a relationship I had developed with the president of a British company, the name of which I can no longer remember. At the time, I was looking for a product and had written to a company in England to ask if they could make it available to us in Canada. The company's president, Dr. Jim Burton, took the time to write me a personal letter informing me he did not have the product. Then he directed me to the product's manufacturer, one of his competitors. It was a simple gesture of kindness but one I have found to be extremely rare in the often-impersonal business world. In my experience, these simple human connections are just as important as anything else that goes into making a business successful. More proof of that came when Jim telephoned me out of the blue several years later to ask if I remembered him. "I certainly do," I said immediately, thinking back to that letter he wrote. "I remember you did something extraordinary. You voluntarily gave a stranger helpful advice."

On this occasion, Jim was calling me in his capacity as the United Kingdom's managing director of a branch of a Spanish ophthalmic company called Cusi. He also represented Cusi in Canada and he wanted to know whether I would be interested in being Cusi's distributor in this country. I was interested – mainly because we did not produce ophthalmic products. We agreed to market these products and also agreed to develop new formulas for the UK market. This arrangement provided us with a valuable opportunity to utilize Canadian patents laws and our research and development capabilities, and to apply all our experience and expertise to selling ophthalmics in the European market.

In the mid-1990s, we were enjoying a significant advantage in the European marketplace, which had come about because Western European governments, in their faulty wisdom, had enacted legislation that made it impossible for a European pharmaceutical company to do research on a drug for which a patent still existed. For a European company to do this was considered a contravention of the existing patent.

Obviously, this gave the rest of the world a huge opportunity to conduct R&D, stockpile products, and hit the ground running the day after a patent expired. Pharmascience was one of the few North American companies that took full advantage of this legislative loophole and David played a key role in overseeing this new direction, including our decision to partner with a German pharmaceutical company, Alfred E. Tiefenbacher. Together, we developed a business-to-business model whereby Pharmascience and AET registered products and sub-licensed our products to all the large generic houses in Western Europe. This agreement was signed in February 1998 and the relationship is still prospering for both parties.

Our relationship with Jim Burton also helped broaden our base in Europe. After a few years of working with Cusi, Jim called me again late in 1995 at a particularly crucial moment in his career. Cusi Worldwide, including Cusi UK, was being bought by Alcon, a multinational ophthalmic company, and Jim was being forced out of his job. David and I both liked Jim personally and we were sympathetic to his plan to branch out on his own. He was going to start by buying products Alcon was not interested in – non-ophthalmic products – and needed us to invest capital in his new venture. In retrospect, I can see a similarity between Jim's situation and mine when I was forced out of ICN and began Pharmascience with the vitamin lines

ICN was no longer interested in. But, really, it was the personal relationship David and I had nurtured with Jim Burton that mattered most in our reaching our decision. "We trust you," I told Jim on behalf of myself and David. David went to England with Pharmascience's comptroller, Bernard Grossman, and an agreement was reached in February 1996. We bought a seventy-five percent stake in a newly formed company, Dominion Pharmacal, while Jim held the remainder of the stock.

This partnership ended in December 2000 when Jim decided he wanted to retire. We did not want to buy Jim out and continue the business on our own because we had no successor to replace him, so we decided to sell the company. David flew to England to help speed the process along. Eventually, Pliva bought Dominion Pharmacal. To this day, we continue to do business with Pliva as well as with its new owner and parent company in Israel, Teva, which has its own impressive history, one I had the chance to witness firsthand as I watched it grow from its very humble beginnings into the largest generic company in the world.

Today, I cannot help but see Teva's unprecedented growth as a microcosm of Israel's phenomenal success as a nation. My first visit to Israel was in 1959 and, while I would like to say I went strictly for spiritual or even for business reasons, the truth is I went because a friend asked me to. An old B'nai Brith buddy, Bill Miller, had fallen in love with Jessica Gelber, a Montreal girl, and she was intent on taking some time out from their relationship by going to Israel on her own. He was not about to take a chance on losing her, so he followed her to Israel and asked me if I wanted to come along as a kind of chaperone.

It was an interesting experience. There was, for instance, the time the three of us toured all of Israel in a jeep and on one occasion ran out of gas in the Galilee on the road to Tiberius. A black car with five Israeli-Arabs in it stopped and offered to help us. I got in with them and got a lift to the nearest gas station. I never gave this decision a second thought. Now, of course, we all still talk about how different the time was then, how relations between Israelis and Arabs, Israeli-Arabs at any rate, were so much more peaceful and tolerant.

Still, I know there were times when Bill would have preferred it if I made myself scarce. As it turned out, I was probably not much of a chaperone. If I had kept a closer eye on Bill and Jessica. I suspect

Bill's plan to talk her out of her timeout from their relationship might not have worked. They were married not long after that trip and remain now, some fifty years later, a happy couple.

My trip to Israel was not my first time overseas – I had already been to Italy numerous times. Soon after the Second World War, Italy became a popular centre for the production of raw materials for the pharmaceutical industry and I had regularly travelled there on behalf of Winley-Morris to purchase raw materials. Italy had the advantage of having good engineers and good chemists who knew how to synthesize drugs. Besides, the Western powers had relaxed the patent laws in Italy in order to build up industry in the war-ravaged nation. These supportive actions were coupled with concerns about Italy – as well as France – becoming Communist countries.

My trips to Israel were more like labours of love. It was a beautiful, agricultural country with what seemed to me to be unlimited potential. Of course, there were unlimited dangers threatening this new nation too. Israel had already fought two wars – the War of Independence in 1948 and the Sinai Campaign in 1956 – and the country was perpetually under siege by the surrounding Arab nations. During this first trip to Israel, I paid a visit to Assia, which would eventually become Teva. It was a bare-bones operation back then. But most industries in that fledgling nation were small at the time. Meanwhile, Israel, formerly Palestine, was emerging as an industrial force. I remember seeing the tin houses or *marbarots* that the new Jewish refugees, most of whom had been forced out of Arab countries, were living in, and I remember marvelling at the spirit of these new citizens. It was remarkable, the way they were looking so steadfastly to the future, the way they were moving beyond the upheaval of being forced from their homes in Egypt, Syria, and all of North Africa, and also the way they were facing the present threat of daily life in Israel.

As for Assia, its operation consisted of synthesizing raw materials and producing finished dosage forms for Israel's small local market as a response to the Arab boycotts being imposed at the time. I received a very favourable welcome from Nahum Solomon, the president of Assia, a multi-generational Israeli and resident of Jerusalem. I am sure he sensed that my motives were not primarily commercial. I wanted to do whatever I could to help Israel. I am a Zionist, in my own way, and have always had a deep emotional attachment to Israel, but I also knew I did not want to live in Israel. Canada was my home and I was determined to be a success here, first and foremost. But, like so many other Diaspora Jews, I also wanted this new country to prosper and I knew I could help by assisting Israel in building a solid industrial infrastructure.

For instance, I learned from Nahum Solomon about a generic product called Meprobamate that Assia was manufacturing. It was being marketed in North America by Carter-Wallace under its original name, Miltown. Miltown was an early version of all those tranquilizers that were about to become incredibly popular. Frankly, it was not a very powerful preparation. At best, it was a mild relaxant and once I heard Assia was producing Meprobamate I said I would be glad to sell it in Canada. I agreed to purchase 100,000 tablets and when I returned to Montreal I placed the order, paying in advance. But when the tablets arrived, they were all broken. They were too soft and had not survived the transport. It was not until two years later, in 1961, when Roz and I were in Israel on our honeymoon, that the subject of the broken tablets came up again. I went to visit Nahum Solomon and the first thing he said to me was, "I owe you money." "Yes, you do," I said. He paid me $435. That does not sound like much, I know, but it demonstrated to me that I was dealing with a man of integrity.

After he reimbursed me, he invited Roz and me to dinner at a restaurant in Jaffa by the Mediterranean Sea. Actually, it was just a shack on the beach where they served barbequed fish, nothing like the fashionable world-class restaurants that have been built on that location today. The shack was also not exactly what my new bride envisioned as a romantic lunch. Here she was, sitting in the sand, presented with a plate of fish, full of bones, their eyes staring at her, while stray cats surrounded us, hungry for scraps. Roz did not like fish and did not enjoy herself, but my business relationship with Assia (Teva) was sealed. At the same time, I became good friends with Eli Hurwitz and his wife, Dahlia, who was Nahum Solomon's daughter.

How did Teva grow so big, so fast? For a start, it got into the U.S. market at a time when it was very encouraging to burgeoning Israeli companies. Teva had friends in the United States who were dedicated to seeing an Israeli company succeed and were prepared to give a company like Teva the same kind of help I was offering but on an even bigger scale. Like me, American Jews were eager for a way to contribute to the growth of Israel. Teva eventually went public in the United States and, like the little country it represents, it continues to grow exponentially.

Teva's success had everything to do with vision, in particular the vision of Eli Hurwitz. As Nahum got older, the reins of the company passed to his son-in-law Eli, who had begun his career as a dishwasher in Assia's laboratories. It was Eli who arranged for the eventual merger between Assia and Teva. I got a close-up glimpse of Eli at his best in the early 1970s. I was in Eli's office in Ramat Gan, just outside Tel Aviv; he told me Teva was producing intermediates used in synthesizing the drug Cimetidine, which was then sold under the trade name Tagamet by the company SmithKline Beecham. I mentioned that ICN Brazil was also manufacturing Cimetidine for their local market and buying the intermediates from a company in France. Eli said, "We'd like to have that business with ICN in Brazil. Can you call Brazil for me?"

I did and made the introduction for Eli. I asked the questions as Eli entered into negotiations through me. He ended up offering the Brazilian company a better price than they were getting from their French partners. Eli knew exactly what he was doing from the start; he knew he could come up with a better price. I then asked the Brazilian CEO if he had any problem buying from Israel; unfortunately, anti-Israel politics were always a consideration. But the Brazilian CEO said that was not a problem, the deal was made and, in a few years, Eli's new business with ICN Brazil was flourishing.

I also remember meeting with Eli in the Plaza Hotel in New York a week after the 1973 Yom Kippur War. He had, for all intents and purposes, just come out of the Sinai, where he was serving as a tank commander. He had his eye on a small company in the equally small town of Sellersville, Pennsylvania, that was selling Acetaminophen tablets, under private labels, to chain stores in the U.S. I confess I thought this was a waste of Eli's time. "Why do you want to do that?" I asked. "Don't worry," he assured me. "I know what I'm doing. You'll see." Did he ever! That little company turned into Teva U.S. Sadly, Eli died in 2011 and Israel lost a great pioneer, a great entrepreneur, a business leader, and a visionary. I lost a great friend.

I have had the good fortune in my life to be drawn to people like Eli, men and women, entrepreneurs, scientists, philanthropists, who have enriched not only my business but, more important, my life. Early in the 2000s, for instance, a neighbour's knock on my back door introduced me to a brand new part of the world as well as an inspirational personal story. The neighbour was the accountant Joe Schlesinger and he asked if we could chat for a moment. He told me he had a client who was interested in doing business with Pharmascience. His client, Bui Nam, had come to Canada as one of the boat people, fleeing South Vietnam after the Viet Cong had taken over the country from the departing U.S. troops in 1975. In the interim, he had started building a life for himself in Montreal. It was not easy. He owned a motel for a while but closed it because of an economic downturn. As it turned out, he was a pharmacist in his native country and had run the largest pharmaceutical company there before the war, in Ho Chi Minh City, formerly Saigon. At the turn of the twenty-first century, with the country increasingly opening up to the rest of the world, Bui was planning to return to Vietnam and get back into the pharmaceutical business. What he wanted from me was the opportunity to sell four of our formulations. We agreed, providing him with Tylenol-related product formulations on a royalty basis.

Not long after the partnership began, Roz and I ended up taking a cruise to Southeast Asia on the *Seaborne*. Once again I was mixing business and pleasure as I decided to pay a visit to my new associate. Roz and I were in for quite a surprise – it turned out Bui Nam was living in a palace. His home was six stories high, with umpteen servants scurrying all over the place. The decor was wall-to-wall antiques. Roz asked Bui Nam where they had all come from and he explained that he had been traveling through the countryside buying them. Evidently, no one knew what treasures they had. Bui Nam went on to explain that their businesses – he was selling pharmaceuticals, his wife, cosmetics – were doing well. Roz and I looked at each other and, no doubt, thought the same thing: "That is quite the understatement!"

I also remember being surprised, on visiting the Canadian embassy in Vietnam, that the people there knew the name Pharmascience. It seems our company name was prominently displayed on a huge billboard advertising one of our products that Bui Nam's company was selling.

In the end, our business relationship with Bui Nam did not last; however on that and subsequent visits I was struck by the industriousness of the country and the Vietnamese people, the women in particular. They seemed to be working nonstop. They were running everything, including building roads by hand. In some ways the country was still very primitive, but I had a feeling that Vietnam was destined to grow industrially. It reminded me of the work ethic of my father's generation, the capacity to continue despite great adversity. I remember thinking: "These people are going places."

I would be remiss if I did not mention here that my first encounter with Vietnamese ingenuity coincided with my first meeting with Thomas Hecht of Continental Pharma. This was in the late 1960s. Back then, Tom and Continental Pharma were importing an experimental anti-tuberculosis product called Isoxyl, which was, as it happened, developed by a Vietnamese prince, Professor N.P. Buu-Hoi, who worked for Continental Pharma SA in Belgium. Tom subsequently appointed Winley-Morris as the exclusive Canadian distributor of Isoxyl. But there was much more to the story than that.

Tom met Prince Buu Loc, the last prime minister of Indochina and the first cousin of the emperor of Vietnam, Bao Dai, in Nice, Vichy France in 1941. Buu Loc brought his cousin, Prince Buu-Hoi, a renowned member of the French National Research Council, to Continental Pharma, where he headed the company's research activities.

It is noteworthy that Tom and his family were fleeing Europe, escaping from the Nazis, when they met and established a close friendship with Prince Buu-Loc. The Hecht family was aided in leaving Nazi-dominated Europe by the intervention of the Portuguese Consul in Bordeaux, France, General De Sousa Mendes, who helped thousands of Jewish refugees secure Portuguese transit visas. De Sousa Mendes is recognized in Jerusalem by the Holocaust Memorial authority, Yad Vashem, as Righteous Among the Nations. The Hecht family settled in Montreal.

It was Tom, while vacationing in Sicily in 1970, who heard that there was a company manufacturing another anti-tuberculosis agent, Ethambutol. He brought it to my attention and we were able to import the raw material before the patent was issued in Canada. We imported enough material to last us a number of years and were able to obtain a good share of the Canadian market for the drug. As for Tom and me, we have maintained a valued and meaningful friendship since our first business association.

When I came back to Montreal after my first trip to Vietnam, I was convinced we had to start a company of our own there and so we arranged for one of our Montreal administrative assistants, a Vietnamese-born woman, Hien Nguyen, to divide her year between Montreal and Ho Chi Minh City where she would serve as our liaison. We obtained our commercial license in February 2006 and our representative office was opened the following year. We continue to do business in Vietnam, although we have not yet had the success we anticipated. But we are continuing to look for new opportunities. Our latest breakthrough in the region has come with our expansion into South Korea, which is set to get going in 2014. Once again, David has taken the lead on this initiative, making a deal with the Seoul-based Korea Kolmar Holdings Co. Ltd, South Korea's largest cosmetics manufacturer. The plan, as reported in the *Montreal Gazette*, is for "the two companies to seek Korean regulatory approval to sell bio-equivalent drugs to treat a variety of psychiatric disorders."

This joint venture, as David explained in an interview with the *Gazette*, "will give us a significant presence in the Korean market and the local expertise in this partnership is a key asset." David also pointed out that this project "is part of [Pharmascience's] strategy to expand internationally and raise the volume of exports from [our] Montreal plant." Thanks to David, our international dealings continue to encourage us to believe in the potential of Pharmascience's global future.

◆

I have already said repeatedly that Roz can attest to the fact that in our travels around the world, including our honeymoon, I always took advantage of the opportunity to mix business with pleasure. But it is worth noting that the one place it was always a pleasure to travel to was Israel. Indeed, it was more than that – it was a privilege, particularly as a Jew, to see that small, beleaguered nation grow into a shining example of progress and promise in the region.

It has been my good fortune as well to witness, firsthand, what the establishment of Israel has meant to Jewish and world history. It has compelled the world to recognize that Jews are entitled, at long last, after 2,000 years of wandering, to their birthright, their place to belong. What a remarkable and moving accomplishment.

Going Home Again

First, they came for the socialists, and I didn't speak out because I wasn't a socialist. Then they came for the trade unionists and I didn't speak out because I wasn't a trade unionist. Then they came for the Jews and I didn't speak out because I wasn't a Jew. Then they came for me and there was no one left to speak for me.

Martin Niemoller

While my attachment to Israel always had me looking to the country's future, my attachment to the Ukraine began with my deep roots in the past. Which was, needless to say, a far from happy past. In the second decade of the twentieth century, when my parents left Russia and made the arduous journey to North America, they were escaping persecution and seeking a land of opportunity for themselves and, more importantly, their children. They could never have foreseen the depth of the terrors they were fleeing.

The worst of these lay in store for my Grandmother Vallie, my mother's mother. When the Second World War started, her grown daughters, Golda and Hava, who lived in the nearby city of Kiev, urged her to move from the small Ukrainian village of Zvenyhorodka to come live with them. But tragically Vallie, like so many others, waited too long and was trapped by the advancing German military forces. For a brief time she managed to find refuge in a neighbour's underground food cellar. But then the Ukrainian family hiding her received a chilling warning from the Ukrainian police: anyone sheltering Jews would be executed. The enthusiasm of the local police for rounding up Jews could not be underestimated and Vallie was left with no choice – she had to set out on her own. My grandmother slipped out of her final shelter and was soon captured, along with many others, and executed in an isolated forest. She died there in 1941, in what was only one of many war-time massacres in the Ukraine. The most infamous of these was the massacre at Babi Yar in which, on 29–30 September 1941, the remaining Jews in Kiev, 33,000 men, women, and children, were rounded up by the Nazis and their Ukrainian collaborators, taken to a ravine at the edge of the city, and shot. Babi Yar would become the general term for similar massacres throughout the Ukraine.

One of my mother's two brothers, Motel, a professor and a mathematician, was killed fighting in the Soviet army in the first days of the German invasion. He had been called up to the front immediately and was never heard from again. My other uncle, Mechel, was also a soldier, but he survived the war. Most of my aunts and cousins were exiled to the Soviet interior, to Tashkent, the capital of the republic of Uzbekistan, one of the main Muslim regions in what was then the Soviet Union. Most of my mother's family were sent there for safety, but they found it a place of punishing hardship.

We were not aware of any of this until the war was over, although my mother had always feared the worst. Only when we finally heard from Mechel did she learn of her mother's death as well as her brother's. She also heard about the plight of her sisters and her nephews and nieces and how bad things continued to be for them. My Uncle Mechel had written to ask his sister Ethel for a winter coat. He was freezing. He was also hungry. My mother sent the coat, the first of her parcels to her family in the Soviet Union. She sent them at least four times a year, purchasing items from the ABC Store on St. Lawrence Boulevard. The idea was not only to send things they could use, like warm clothing, but, more important, extra things that they could sell or barter for money or food.

Finally, in 1962, my mother had the chance to visit her family. She went to Kiev, the capital of the Ukraine, for three weeks and I remember that when she returned, the Canadian customs agent asked what she was bringing into the country and she answered in Russian. She had spoken only Russian and Yiddish on her trip and was no doubt experiencing a kind of culture shock. For her, it must have seemed as if she was stepping back in time to the day in 1924 when she had immigrated to Canada with my father and my sister Luba.

Of course, my mother's return to the Ukraine was profoundly emotional. Mechels's son, my first cousin Valentine (Val) was there when my mother arrived, so I will let him pick up the story:

My Aunt Ethel's arrival was something special. Imagine the whole *mespocha* [family] waiting for her on the tarmac. There were no gates at airports then. We were just waiting near where the plane landed. That was the European style, then. The plane arrived and you were practically next to it. Who was there that day? Better ask: who wasn't? There were the surviving siblings, my father, her brother, and her two sisters, Golda and Hava. As well as a huge contingent of cousins: maybe forty people altogether, myself included. So the plane lands and we notice a small, small lady coming down the airplane stairway. Remember, it had been forty-five years since they'd all seen each other and my father and my aunts say, almost in unison, "There, there, she is! That's Ethel!" How did they know her? I couldn't say. But I witnessed that. I also remember my father and I went into the room when she was being interviewed by the Soviet custom agents. She saw her brother, my father, and though she had last seen him when he was a boy of ten – he was fifty-six now – she recognized him right away. She just looked at him and said, "The eyes, the eyes, they never change."

We did our best to try to help her get through customs quickly and smoothly but what you have to remember about Soviet customs agents then was that they did not work alone. The dreaded secret police or KGB was always by their side, giving orders, pursuing their agenda. She had just arrived and was struggling with their questions, struggling with her Russian. I knew a few words in English so I tried to help out. But when I did I heard an intimidating voice behind me saying, "Young man, you don't need to do that." This was not a customs agent speaking. This was KGB. The point is that they were not making things easy for her on purpose. She was understandably under a lot of stress. But then, when she was explaining who all the gifts she had brought from Canada were for, she said to one of the customs agents, "Here, this is for you." She handed the agent one of the wrapped presents. This was very clever of her, of course. She had been away a long time, but not so long she had forgotten how our part of the world works. After that, we were all allowed to leave.

The visit was hard and emotional for my mother and it was made more difficult by the strictures put on her by typical Soviet bureaucratic paranoia. (Something I would experience, too, some years later when I visited.) She was not allowed, for example, to travel to the site of her mother's death. As Val recalled:

We had applied to go to the gravesite near Zyvenyhorodka, but the officials came up with one excuse after another. In fact, we were told we should discourage her from making the trip. "Tell her," they said, "that there are no hotels there, no plane. Tell her, it's not a good time to go. Tell her, she can't take her family with her." Our plan was to rent a car, to make it a day trip, and to have her accompanied by one other person. But still she was told no. Aunt Ethel made it easy on all of us and said we shouldn't worry. She said she would go to the gravesite the next time she came. Of course, there would be no next time. There was one great night, though. She had been forced to stay at a hotel and not with any of her relatives, but one night she came to my father's apartment and the whole family was there. It was a big party, a big reunion. She felt, finally, like she was home.

My mother's commitment to her family, despite such great distances and the obstacles put in her way, was a testament to the importance of family in her life. You can live around the corner from your closest relatives and the relationship can be as fragile as glass. Or, as in my mother's case, you can live halfway around the world and it can remain an unbreakable bond. I had learned that lesson as a young man, watching my mother sending parcels to her family in the Ukraine year after year. When she died, some six years after that trip to see her family again, Roz and I kept the tradition of sending parcels going. But I was curious to meet these people I had never met. I was also worried that out of sight was out of mind. I was afraid that if Roz and I did not have a direct, personal connection with these people we would be inclined to stop sending parcels. So in 1973 Roz and I traveled to Kiev.

To say that it was an interesting trip is putting it mildly. Almost as soon as we arrived, our relatives started showing up at our hotel. There were the predictable warm greetings but there was also a certain reticence on their part. I noticed that as each person came in to our room to see us, they were pointing to the ceiling. The message was clear: we had to be careful of what we said because in the Soviet Union you could be sure there was always someone listening.

There were also guards on every floor of the hotel and it soon became clear to me what their function was: whenever Roz and I left the room, the guards would go into our room and go through our baggage. This was our rather rude introduction to a police state.

Indeed, our time in the Soviet Union was an eye-opener for us. And while I have hardly ever traveled anywhere without entertaining some thought of doing business there, I can say, with confidence, I had no such thoughts on this visit.

Probably the most memorable part of the trip occurred when Roz and I were invited to a family dinner, one that echoed the big family dinner held eleven years earlier for my mother. This time the family congregated in my Aunt Hava's small apartment. It was so small I wondered how she would be able to accommodate us, let alone all the other relatives and friends who kept showing up. But everyone took this inconvenience in stride. They were used to making do. They just took one of the doors in the apartment off its hinges so it could serve as a long dining room table. It was during that evening that my Uncle Mechel took me out into the hall – he knew enough to not talk freely, even in his sister's home – and whispered in Yiddish to me that he wanted to come visit me in Canada. The trip took some arranging but it happened a year later. In a way, his arrival in Montreal was badly timed since he came just as I was scheduled to take a month-long ICN-sponsored management course at Harvard University. At first, Uncle Mechel and Roz had some problems communicating as he spoke only Russian and Yiddish and Roz spoke neither. But they ended up managing. Mechel spent a lot of time visiting Montreal's Jewish Public Library. There he found books he could not read or even get access to at home – like Aleksandr Solzhenitsyn's acclaimed saga of Soviet repression, *The Gulag Archipelago*. Mechel stayed three months and before he left he had already come to the decision that he would immigrate to Canada with his family the first chance he got. Here is his son Val's recollection of his father's return to the Soviet Union:

> He had a wonderful time in Montreal and when he got home, we had a get-together. Everyone was in my apartment this time, asking him, "So what do you think of Canada?" He didn't say anything. He just pointed up at the ceiling. He never trusted anything. He would not speak freely in any room. But we lived next to a 1,000-year-old forest and he and I went for a walk. I said, "So, Papa, tell me what is it really like?" He just looked at me and said, "If you go, I'll go too." From then on, whenever anyone asked if there were opportunities in Canada, he would say no. But, in private, when he knew no one was listening, he would say, "Yes, the opportunities are incredible."

It would take a while for Mechel to realize this dream. His eldest son, Joseph, immigrated to Canada first with his family. He was a butcher by trade and I helped him find a job at a kosher butcher shop in Toronto. That was in the late 1970s. But it was in the early 1980s that things really began to change in the Soviet Union, especially for Jews. Here is Val again:

I put in an application for me and my family in 1979, but for two years we were refused. We were just told, "We are not ready to let you go." That's all. However, the moment Ronald Reagan came to power in 1980, we knew things had changed. We knew the Soviets would never work with Reagan's predecessor, Jimmy Carter, but, with Reagan, we knew our time was coming. We knew we would be able to leave soon. The Soviets were afraid of Reagan. He was such a strong personality. They knew they could not match him. I came here in 1981, on October 26th, to be precise. A day I will never forget. We were among forty families that were allowed to go. It was like the Soviet government was saying to the West, "Here, do you want some Jews?" We knew we would get just one chance. They would call and say, "Are you ready to leave?" And we had to be ready.

I was thirty-four when I came to Canada. I came with my wife, my parents, and my children. But we had to leave my wife's parents behind. They had to sign a pledge to the KGB that they were against us going. It was a kind of bureaucratic torture. The government wanted to make sure we paid a price, a big one, for leaving. The pledge, a false one of course, that my in-laws were forced to sign seemed to assure that they would never be allowed to leave the Soviet Union. It meant that, as far as they knew, they would never see their children or grandchildren again. That was a huge sacrifice they made for us.

As it turned out, it would be another decade before Val's wife, Ella, saw her parents again. By then, Val was able to sponsor them and they came to Canada. Val, a civil engineer by trade, was not able to find work here in his field and eventually came to work for Pharmascience in sales. Many years later, Val's son, Boris, who had studied at McGill and Harvard and earned his PhD in microbiology, would come to work at Pharmascience too, and become a director in the company. Boris married Debbie Finkelberg – Jonathan's wife Dana's first cousin – and they have two children. Boris's twin sister, Elana, an advertising executive, has also flourished in her new country. She is married to Michel Bendayan and they also have two children.

As I said, I had never entertained any plans to do business in the Ukraine or visit it again. However, when it became clear in the early 1990s that the Soviet Union, under Mikhail Gorbachev, was about to collapse, my views on doing business in Russia changed practically overnight. It was also around this time that I received a phone call from Abraham Katzellenbogen, known to everyone in the community simply as Mr. Bogen. He worked at the local JIAS office (the Jewish Immigration Aid Society), an organization that helps Jews settle productively in Canada and throughout the world. Mr. Bogen explained that he had a visitor, a fellow named Pavel Melekhov, who worked in the Soviet pharmaceutical industry and had just arrived in Canada from Vienna. He wanted to stay in this country and was in desperate need of a sponsor.

Eventually, he would need a job, too, and Mr. Bogen wondered if I could meet with him. I met with Pavel (Paul) and I learned that he had been director of operations for all the plants producing antibiotics in the USSR. At the time, we did not have a job commensurate with his skill and experience. I explained to him that Pharmascience was still a relatively small operation – this was February 1991 – and we dealt with finished goods, not the production of raw materials, which was Paul's area of expertise. In fact, all I could offer him back then was a position as an inventory clerk. To say he was overqualified would be a vast understatement. Still, I explained he could take this job with the understanding that if something more suitable to his skills opened up, he would be considered. To his credit, Paul did not hesitate. He accepted the inventory clerk job.

"My interview with Morris was just a few weeks after I arrived in Canada. So I had nothing in my pockets," as Paul recounts the story. "I needed a job. But I also felt, meeting Morris, talking to him, that there was room for advancement in Pharmascience. I'm sure when Morris hired me he already thought there was something that was going to happen in the Soviet Union. Of this, I am completely sure."

Here, Paul is mistaken. I have never been adept at historical or political prognostications. I had no clue that circumstances in Eastern Europe, and particularly the Soviet Union, were about to change so dramatically and that that change would also have a dramatic impact on Paul and Pharmascience. Still, it is true that the collapse of the

Gorbachev-led Soviet Union, not long after Paul had come to work for Pharmascience, opened the doors wide to doing business in what appeared to be a new Russia. I conferred with Paul and asked if he would be interested in returning home and connecting with his old contacts in the industry. His response was pragmatic. "Yes," he said, "if we can do business there, I'd be happy to go back."

We made a deal; Paul would divide his year in two, working six months in Russia and the other six months in Canada, where his wife, Irina Tsyskovskaia, and their young son, Denis, remained. Almost immediately, David, Paul, and I went to St. Petersburg, the former Leningrad and Paul's birthplace, where we opened our office. In a few months, Paul was able to secure an order from the Russian military for an antibiotic called Cefazolin Injectable. Paul still has photos of himself posing with David, me, and high-ranking scientists from the famous Pasteur Institute. But, despite this good start, Russia was an unstable country, experiencing a great deal of chaos and lawlessness. It was the Eastern European equivalent of the Wild Wild West. I remember receiving a phone call from Paul early in this venture during which he said, "I'm not comfortable working in this environment." He did not feel safe, and for good reason, so we decided to move the operation to Kiev. The situation was not great in the Ukraine either, but it was better. It turned out I still had a cousin, the husband of a cousin, there who held a senior position in the Ministry of Health. So we made what we thought was an arrangement with my cousin, but it only took one day to discover that he could not be trusted. Paul, then, decided to operate on his own and established his new Kiev office on the campus of a university hospital. We incorporated our Ukrainian company on 24 November 1994.

"Why a hospital?" I asked him.

"Because that's where you have the best security," Paul explained. Security guards patrolled the exterior of the hospital twenty-four hours a day and Paul had a steel door installed to safeguard his office. Here is Paul explaining why we were so successful in this region so quickly and why we have continued to be successful:

> We started to do business in Kiev because there was a tradition of manufacturing there. Even so, there was, at this time, when we were beginning, a complete collapse of the medical and the pharmaceutical industry ... In the next few years the economic situation gradually began to improve and finally we could sell products

we manufactured here in Canada. Now, we employ more than seventy people, most of whom are medical doctors. It's a big office in Kiev. We are the only Canadian company that has an office like this in the Ukraine. We are also a legal entity and we have all the required licenses to manufacture our products and also export them to Russia, to Moldova, Lithuania, Georgia, many of the former republics.

Business is growing. Of course, these are still very risky places – Russia, Ukraine, all these newly established countries. We were lucky. I was also very careful. When we started the business I told Morris that my number one priority was not to lose money. But we started making money from the first year, supplying antibiotics to the army as well as the Ministry of Health. Why were we successful? It was important that I happened to speak Russian better than English. I also understood how to avoid risks, problems. A lot of people there try to take advantage of foreigners. For them a foreigner is someone to be cheated. For me, it was a matter of knowing the rules of the game. The rules are this: first, don't trust any promises; second, rely on your good will and your knowledge of how to run a profitable business.

I also must add that in my life I was lucky enough to meet a lot of talented people, in both the Soviet Union and Canada, but never in my life have I met such a person as Morris Goodman. Apart from his entrepreneurial talents, he is a very gifted scientist. One of the best scientific minds I have ever met, in fact. It's not a coincidence the name science is in the name of his company. Morris is very logical. Maybe he doesn't know mathematics or physics as a professor might, but he does have an absolutely methodological way of thinking. I also know that a lot of people work for Pharmascience because they are impressed with Morris. I try to follow his behaviour when I am in Ukraine. I am very excited to talk about Morris. Without Morris, Pharmascience would not happen. Without Morris, I would not happen. People who have Morris in their life are happy people.

Paul is far too kind in his praise. It is in large part to his credit today that both the Ukrainian and Canadian governments have put their stamp of approval on our operation. In addition, Paul, from his base in Kiev, is marketing into many surrounding Muslim countries and to all of Eastern Europe, including Lithuania and Estonia. Paul still divides his time between Kiev and Montreal. And his wife, who has a PhD in chemistry, has worked at the University of Montreal and is now working with our regulatory department at Pharmascience. They are both remarkable success stories, not just as far as Pharmascience is concerned but as far as this country is concerned. They are wonderful examples of the possibilities Canada has always offered its citizens and immigrants alike: people like Paul and, for that matter, my parents.

◆

Another thing became possible with the fall of the Soviet Union and Pharmascience's subsequently creating a foothold for itself in Ukraine. In 1994 I got the opportunity to do what my mother had not had the chance to do on her visit to the country of her birth some three decades earlier. I revisited my family's tragic past and traveled to the village where my grandmother had died. One of my first times there, on business in Kiev with David, I met with my first cousin Siena, my Aunt Golda's son, and he, David, Paul Melekhov, and I rented a car and drove to Zvenyhorodka, to the house where my grandmother once lived. There, my cousins managed to explain to the woman living in the house who I was. They asked her if I could look around. She said yes, but there was not much to see. What there was, however, was startling: it was a small place, just a hovel really. I can still remember being amazed by the stove, which was made out of dirt, amazed, moreover, at how people had lived like this and still did. I also wanted to see where my grandmother was buried and so I made the poignant trip my mother had been denied so many years earlier. A villager took us to the forest where my grandmother and her fellow Jews had been executed. Again, there was not much to see, but the sight was chilling nevertheless. There was no monument to what had happened, no dedication as there was at Babi Yar in Kiev, for instance. There was absolutely no recognition in the town of Zvenyhorodka that anything dreadful had occurred there. Nothing to indicate the terrible crime that had taken place on this obscure piece of land where so many had been murdered en masse, killed only because they were Jewish. What was there, though, broke my heart. I saw two mounds of dirt: one for the adults and then, beside the first mound, a smaller one. It was for the innocent children, the children who had been murdered.

13

Investing in People: Two Case Studies

A man should never stop learning.
Maimonides

After all this time, I should be immune to surprises. Indeed, I could probably be forgiven for thinking that when it comes to my business I have seen everything. But the truth is, I have never had this feeling working in the pharmaceutical business. I am continually stimulated, rejuvenated really, by the fresh possibilities, the renewed hope that I feel whenever I learn about a new drug or treatment. Frankly, that is the reason I still come into work every day full of enthusiasm and curiosity, expecting, always, to be pleasantly surprised. Even so, I could never have predicted what happened a few years ago when an old drug, one I had first learned about forty years earlier, resurfaced and was showing exciting – and remarkably promising – results fighting an extremely virulent form of cancer. What is more, the person doing the basic research with this old drug was doing it right here in my own backyard; in fact, she was doing her research at my old alma mater, the University of Montreal.

In the spring of 2009, Roz and I attended a cocktail party at the University of Montreal. The gathering was in honour of my old classmate Jean Coutu and his wife, Marcelle, who were announcing their substantial gift to the University's Institute for Research in Immunology and Cancer (IRIC). Almost as soon as I arrived, I was approached by one of the university's researchers who asked if I had happened to see a paper just published in the medical journal *Blood*. I had yet to read *Blood*, but the day before I had seen a story in the *Montreal Gazette* that was inspired by the article. There had also been a national story on CTV, which I had heard about, with the tantalizing headline "Antiviral Drug Becomes Promising Cancer-Fighter." The gist of the TV broadcast and the newspaper coverage was that eleven patients in Montreal with AML – acute myleloid leukemia – were being treated with the drug Ribavirin. Nothing else had worked for these patients and this treatment was being viewed as a last resort. Despite the seriousness of their condition, the drug was showing remarkable results. According to the CTV story, nine of the patients had improved within a matter of months. The treatment was also distinguishing itself from conventional chemotherapy in that there were no debilitating or dangerous side effects. One patient, Fred Klamph, who was featured on the TV news story, was feeling well enough to travel to Florida and go scuba diving.

The lead researcher, from the University of Montreal, was Dr. Katherine Borden, who was also interviewed. She told CTV news: "In several of the patients, we had remissions, which is completely unheard of for these kinds of patients. And in another subgroup of patients we had really dramatic drops in the number of leukemia cells they had, including patients where we could no longer or barely detect any leukemia in them anymore. To have patients who feel good and can go out and have a life, and not be in hospital, sick all the time, which is often the normal course of leukemia, that was really exciting for us and that's why we're excited."

This story could not help but sound encouraging from a medical point of view. But, for me, there was also a personal aspect to the story. I had first learned about Ribavirin in 1971, during that pivotal period in my life when I was in the process of selling Winley-Morris to Milan Panic and ICN. Ribavirin had been discovered at ICN's research laboratories back then and, as I mentioned earlier, Panic had latched onto it like a lifeline, touting it as a possible cure for the common cold and staking his and ICN's reputation in the stock market on it. It was part of his pitch to me when he was trying to convince me to sell Winley-Morris. Ribavirin proved, of course, not to be a cure for the common cold but, some twenty years later, after I had left ICN, it had resurfaced, this time, when combined with Interferon, as an effective treatment for Hepatitis C. This breakthrough effectively saved ICN and Panic and did so just in the nick of time. As it turned out, it was his lifeline.

So did I know anything about Ribavirin? Yes, you could say Ribavirin and I had a history. Hearing about it at the Coutu cocktail party in this exciting new context was a little like hearing about a long-lost friend who you suddenly learn is back in town and wants to go over old times. So when that University of Montreal researcher asked me if I wanted to be introduced to Dr. Borden, the author of the paper in *Blood*, I said just what you might expect: "Indeed, I have a story to tell her about Ribavirin that I'm certain she knows nothing about."

Dr. Katherine Borden, or Kathy, as I have come to call her, is a native Montrealer who has, in her own words, lived everywhere. She has also spent much of her valuable time doing what even the best researchers are condemned to do: chase after academic grants. Her previous job had been at the prestigious Mount Sinai Hospital in New York and, from there, she had come to the University of Montreal in 2004. Currently, she is a full professor at IRIC and she holds a Canada Research Chair. Like so many of the talented researchers I have met and worked with over the years, she is an impressive woman – down-to-earth and brilliant at the same time. She comes to work in running shoes and spends her days dedicated to solving the most complicated mysteries of illness and mortality. With Ribavirin, she has had the opportunity to perform miracles, to give patients new hope and time they never would have had otherwise. Obviously, this has increased her commitment to her work and, after meeting her, it increased my commitment to helping her in any way I could.

Like most researchers I have met, Kathy is both fiercely dedicated to the task at hand and routinely frustrated by the limitations that invariably place obstacles in the way of her getting on with that task. She was in the midst of dealing with some of those obstacles when we first met and, as Kathy tells it, the timing of our meeting could not have been better. Almost too good to be true is the way Kathy remembers it:

> I'd never met Morris before and someone at the cocktail party came up to me and said this man had a story he wanted to tell me. It turns out he had more than one. He told me all these very entertaining tales about his history with Ribavirin, going back to his selling his company, Winley-Morris, to ICN in the early 1970s. I got the sense, talking to Morris, that he thought of this drug as "the one that got away." So by the end of our talk Morris told me Pharmascience was going to manufacture Ribavirin for our next trial and provide it to me free of charge. Of course, I thought that would be awesome. But I have to tell you that, as a research scientist who goes to a lot of these

sort of cocktail parties, I know that there are a lot of people who come up to you and offer you all sorts of things, but then you never hear from them again. Previous life experience told me the same would probably turn out to be true in this case. But then I didn't know Morris yet. He really came through. His decision to contribute the drug to my research has been a real bonus. At the time, it was a lifeline, really. If Morris hadn't come on board when he did, this research might have all stopped. It has certainly made a lot of our work possible. Patients are now taking the drug made at Pharmascience ... taking it for leukemia.

Our dream now is to see how Ribavirin works when it is given to patients much earlier on. It's only been used as a last resort drug up to now. Now, we want to get it approved, perhaps in combination with another drug, and move forward with patients in earlier stages of the disease.

In addition to providing Kathy with the Ribavirin she needs for the clinical studies being done by Dr. Wilson Miller Jr and Dr. Sarit Assouline at the Segal Centre of the Jewish General Hospital, I have also been able to assist Kathy with other matters. For instance, she is now doing research into combining Ribavirin with Cytarabine, an older drug used in traditional chemotherapy. The key here is to keep the doses of Cytarabine low, so it can be effective but also not cause the usual side effects. As a consequence, patients can take this treatment at home. This combination is also something Kathy will be able to take out a patent on; something she cannot do if Ribavirin is administered on its own. As a consequence, I have had Pharmascience's intellectual property lawyers working on obtaining a patent for this aspect of her research, which, if successful, would entail the University of Montreal receiving royalties. If the treatment can be approved it can be given to patients at an earlier stage in their disease.

The kind of research Kathy Borden is engaged in is comparable to running a marathon. The good news is that she recently sent me an email informing me that she has been awarded a three-year grant, totalling $600,000, from the U.S. Leukemia and Lymphoma Society (LLS). This award amounts to an enormous vote of confidence in the work she is doing. More to the point, it means she can keep doing that work, which is to say continue her trials. According to Kathy, it is just that simple: "No money, no trial!"

But another email I recently received from Kathy summed up for me my lifelong commitment to research, and why Pharmascience's motto has always been "To make a difference." Kathy was writing to bring me up to date on the latest news about Ribavirin and told me about a young girl in San Diego who had developed AML after receiving chemotherapy to treat her neuroblastoma when she was only five months old. She is two now and had failed to improve after at least two rounds of chemotherapy. Her father recently approved starting her on Ribavirin. After just three days, her blood work showed remarkable results. And while her father knows this treatment is a long shot, he told Kathy that he was grateful for Ribaviran because he could not bear to give his daughter another painful and likely ineffective round of chemo. He was desperate to try something that would not make her so terribly sick. The hope was that Ribavirin may make her well enough, and provide her with enough time, that she can one day receive a bone marrow transplant. This desperate father was, understandably, looking for a miracle and, while Ribavirin may not be a miracle drug yet, it did one miraculous thing: it gave this man, and his young daughter, hope where there was none before.

Kathy Borden and the Jewish General Hospital continue their clinical research with Ribavirin. Their results recently attracted the attention of CTV producers and Kathy and I were asked to appear on the national morning program, Canada AM, to discuss Kathy's research.

At the same time, unknown to me, a new drug, Sofosbuvir, was working its way through the Health Canada regulatory system on its way to being approved for sale as an oral treatment for Hepatitis C. It would be the first oral preparation for this disease, replacing the previous long-time treatment of choice, Interferon. Like Interferon, Sofosbuvir requires Ribavirin to have maximum effectiveness. However, Ribavirin tablets are currently approved only in a kit form along with Interferon. Following our television appearance, Pharmascience was contacted and asked to make a submission to Health Canada to get a Notice of Compliance to market Ribavirin as a separate drug. We expect to have the drug on the market by early 2015.

The story of Ribavirin that started for me in 1971, after I sold my small company to ICN, is still making an impact on my life in 2013. Can it get more exciting?

When it comes to business, I admit I have been too cautious at times, too reluctant to roll the so-called dice. My affiliations with entrepreneurs and corporate players like Milan Panic or Shaul Eisenberg have demonstrated to me that I am not that kind of swashbuckling businessman. However, when it comes to taking chances on people, I have operated very differently. For example, from the moment I met Kathy Borden, from the moment she began to tell me about her work, I knew I was going to bet on her and assist her in any way I could.

Of course, with Kathy, I was backing a research project as opposed to a business enterprise. In contrast, my introduction to Ronald Reuben two decades ago started out looking like a huge business risk. In 1992, Roz and I were on our way to Florida when I received a call from Michael Cape, who was running Marcelle Cosmetics. I have known Michael a long time and Roz went to high school with his wife, Pearl. In fact, Pearl and Michael and Roz and I were married on the same evening and we spent part of our honeymoons together on our way to Europe in 1961 on the *Empress of Britain*.

Now, Michael was phoning in a response to a request from Barry Shapiro, a lawyer, trying to help this Reuben kid out – Ronald was probably twenty-four at the time. Ronald was about to lose the business he had started to his partner. Indeed, it appeared that Medicom, a company that dealt in medical and dental supplies, was about to be taken right out from under him. It was a complicated situation but the gist of it was, as Michael Cape explained to me, that young Mr. Reuben was in a tough spot. All this was happening to him at a time when his mother was not well. He had grown up in Israel and his father had left when he was young so he had no parent to talk to. I called Ronald from a pay phone at the airport in Montreal and he explained that he did not have "the financial resources to retain ownership of Medicom." I asked him how much money he needed. He said $200,000. He sounded both sincere and sincerely in trouble. Relying on my respect for Barry Shapiro and Michael Cape and for their sound judgment in this matter, I contacted our finance people and asked them to transfer the money Ronald required to his account. I decided I could check into the situation once I returned from my vacation in Florida. I do not remember much about the phone call, but Ronald understandably does. Here is his version:

I had just gone through a year of acrimony with my partner. I had also put everything I had into Medicom. I mean I didn't even finish university. I dropped my last course at McGill to start

the business. I had nothing else. I was at my wit's end. And then
Morris called and said, "I understand there is a need." I told him
my story very briefly on the phone. I remember he didn't say a
word. He was just listening for the longest time. Then he finally
said, "Let me see what I can do." What Morris did was invest
in Medicom in the form of a $200,000 loan. He said that when
Medicom paid that back we would become partners – 50-50.
This money was enough to pay off the other partner. I remember
I showed up at a meeting with Medicom's lawyers with a cheque
from Morris – I still hadn't met Morris, by the way – and I put
the money on the table and these guys were floored. They never
expected me to be able to come up with the money. In fact, they
had counted on me not being able to come up with the money.

When I returned from Florida, I realized that things were worse
for Ronald Reuben and for Medicom than I had thought. My impulsive good will gesture had led me straight into a financial mess of
someone else's making. It was a mess that surprised Ronald too. Here,
he is recalling an extremely difficult time in his life:

I had audited the statements and I knew Medicom wasn't doing
great, but it was okay. Or so I thought. But once I took charge
of the business, I learned, as I looked more and more into the ac-
counting, that we were losing money and, more than that, the
business was technically bankrupt. And I was the sap who had
just bought it. Not only that, I had pulled in Morris, a guy who
I'd never seen, and dragged him into a lot of trouble. I remember
I first met with him before Passover and I had to tell him the
truth about the company's finances. We were sitting in the Pharmascience offices and Morris blew a gasket. I was twenty-four
and I felt horrible. My credibility was down to nothing. I looked
like a thief. How could I not know my own finances? What I did-
n't know, of course, was that while I was concentrating on sales
on the outside, my partner was on the inside, cooking the books.
I was shaking by the time the meeting with Morris and his people
was finally over. I was feeling lower than dirt. Which was when
Morris called me over and said: "By the way, what are you doing
for Passover?" I told him I was alone here in Montreal. So he
said, "Come over to my house for the Seder." I still remember
that and, still, whenever I retell the story, the hair stands up on

the back of my head. Morris showed me kindness like no other person had. But that is one of his traits. He can be hard as a whip. He can zero in on a problem or an issue right away. But I remember most of all this simple act of kindness. From that time on, I had only one thing in mind: I wanted to earn his trust, repay his kindness.

Ronald was determined to return my investment and he worked hard to make that happen. "All right," I said to Ronald, "are you ready to roll up your sleeves? If so Bernie Grossman (Pharmascience's CFO) and I will come into your office once a week to help you run your business." And for the next year, Ronald was in the office from five in the morning until one in the morning. His business was all he cared about. He had a lot of scars. He had seen a lot of the ugly side of the business world and I was trying to build up his confidence. I was taking the time to show him how to run a successful business. I was also showing him that I trusted him. The result was that Medicom eventually grew into a very successful business. It went from the brink of bankruptcy to a company with $200 million in sales, doing business in North America, Europe, and Asia. Medicom celebrated its twenty-fifth anniversary in 2013. In addition, in 2003, Ronald was presented with the Federation CJA's 2003 Sam Steinberg Award as "Young Jewish Entrepreneur of the Year" and in September 2013 received the Ernst & Young Entrepreneur of the Year Award for Quebec.

I am also proud to say that Ronald, now married to Miriam Dahan, a dentist, and with two children, Emma and Aiden, views me as a role model who helped him put his life back together as both a businessman and a family man.

"Morris Goodman changed my life," Ronald has been kind enough to say of our relationship. "I don't just owe a lot to this man, I owe everything to him. I know he has built a reputation for himself as a philanthropist in recent years, but I feel like his philanthropy also extends to me; that it started with me in a way. I am a product of it. In any case, the bottom line, for Morris, is kindness. He didn't need to be kind to me, but he was. He didn't need to believe in me, but he did. And it's made all the difference."

Just in case you are starting to think my track record in betting on people is perfect, let me correct that notion. I can relate two other case studies that could not have turned out more differently than those of Kathy and Ronald. Many years ago, a secretary at Pharmascience asked me to co-sign a loan for her at the bank. She was borrowing money to buy a house with her husband. A month later they declared bankruptcy and I ended up paying the bank. I was never repaid.

Another time, one of the congregants at the Shaar Hashomayim, whom I did not know personally, came to my office at Pharmascience and asked me for a loan. He said he was in desperate financial straits. As I was vice-president of the Shaar at the time, I felt an obligation to be more trusting and more charitable than I might otherwise have been. I loaned him $10,000. He gave me post-dated cheques, all of which bounced. I was never paid back. He still comes to the synagogue but surprisingly never says a word to me when I see him.

But while I am disappointed by some of the mistakes in judgment I have made, the satisfaction of the success stories far outweighs any regrets I might have. I keep on trusting in people, learning from them, and investing in them, both financially and personally. The thing is, I know that if I had let the bad experiences influence my faith in people, it would be my own quality of life, as well as the satisfaction I get from giving, that would be severely diminished.

14

Making a Difference

We make a living by what we get; we make a life by what we give.
                              Attributed to Winston Churchill

From the start of my career, my success in the pharmaceutical business has been inextricably tied to the evolution of the generic drug business. I have watched that industry grow and have participated in its growth, not just in terms of its commercial viability but in terms of its respectability and expanding value to society. Remember, I was labeled a "pirate" by the multinationals when I started selling generics in the 1950s and 1960s. By the 1990s, though, the landscape was changing dramatically and I am proud of the role Pharmascience has played and continues to play in the transformation of the drug business.

We were, for instance, involved in one particularly trailblazing effort, one orchestrated by the giant multinational Eli Lilly. Based in Indianapolis, Eli Lilly was founded 137 years ago and is now the tenth largest pharmaceutical company in the world. In 1996, though, Lilly faced a significant and ultimately wide-reaching challenge. The company was about to lose its patent protection in Canada on its ground-breaking anti-depressant Fluoxetine, which is better known by its trade name, Prozac. In 1974 Fluoxetine was discovered to be an effective treatment for depression as well as conditions such as obsessive-compulsive disorder, bulimia, anorexia, and other panic disorders. Early on, it was apparent that Prozac was more than just another drug. For better, and sometimes for worse, it captured the spirit of the time, one marked by an unrelenting desire for self-improvement. Prozac inspired bestselling books – *Listening to Prozac* and *Prozac Nation* – that were either for or against it; it also established a place for itself in the popular culture as the first of its kind – the first, that is, in a new wave of so-called "happiness" drugs. As a result of all this, Prozac also enjoyed enormous brandname success in the marketplace. But by the 1990s, with the patent ending, Eli Lilly's Canadian president, Nelson Sims, was determined that Prozac not be overtaken by the generic market, at least not without developing a new strategy to prevent this from happening. In this respect, Sims and Lilly broke ranks with the other multinationals: rather than fight the growing generic industry, Eli Lilly decided to join it. Sims made the calculation that Lilly was better off profiting from the generic business than losing ninety percent of its profits once the patent ran out. It would take some time and some convincing but eventually all the multinationals would follow the model that Lilly started in Canada with Prozac. In this regard, Nelson Sims was a trailblazer.

This also explains how Sims began looking for a Canadian partner for Prozac and ended up approaching Pharmascience. Even so, I knew we were not his first choice; I knew that he had considered other Canadian companies before us. Doing so was understandable since, at the time, we were probably only the fifth or sixth largest generic drug company in the country. To be honest, I still do not know for sure why we were ultimately chosen. If I had to guess, I would say that Nelson Sims chose Pharmascience because he believed that we were trustworthy and that we would do what we said we were going to do. He had as evidence our solid reputation in the marketplace. In the end, I guess you could say he found in Pharmascience a fit that suited him. It suited us, too, and then some.

Simply put, it is impossible to overestimate what it meant to us – a relatively small and young company – to sign the distribution agreement in June 1995 and have the rights to bring out the generic version of Prozac. After all, Prozac was one of the top ten drugs being prescribed in Canada at the time. Furthermore, we were going to be able to bring out our product a full four months before Lilly's patent on Prozac ended. What this head start meant is that every pharmacy in the country would be compelled to buy a bottle of Pharmascience's pms-Fluoxetine from us.

There were also ancillary benefits that accompanied our partnership with Eli Lilly. Almost immediately, we were able to partner with ten other multinationals based on the fact that we had been Lilly's choice for Prozac. My son Jonathan, who was twenty-six years old at the time and had joined Pharmascience as vice-president in charge of business development, worked diligently on seven of these deals and was instrumental in consumating the deal with Lilly.

Some of the other prominent companies we ended up representing included AstraZeneca, Novartis, Alcon, Roche, Fournier, Schering-Plough, Purdue Pharma, and Janssen Pharmaceuticals, a division of Johnson & Johnson. All of this is to say that our association with Eli Lilly was more than just a business deal; in the end, it dramatically changed the face of Pharmascience. It provided us with more than business: it gave us the intangibles of power, prestige, and credibility.

Our excitement about this change in our fortunes was probably summed up best by Sheila McGovern, a business reporter for the *Montreal Gazette*, who said in an article dated 15 April 1996:

> They're feeling great at Montreal-based Pharmascience. They've got Prozac. Of course, they're not taking the blockbuster antidepressant. They're selling it – in its generic form ... in the same green-and-cream capsules as the drug's creator, Eli Lilly – for 25% less than the original.
>
> But unlike other Canadian generic manufacturers, Pharmascience isn't locked in a legal battle with Eli Lilly, which obtained an interim injunction banning all look-alike generics from the market. In fact, Pharmascience has Eli Lilly's blessing. It is all the other generics that are not so thrilled.

As I said, she got it right. This was a thrilling time.

I mentioned that Jonathan's arrival at Pharmascience coincided with the Lilly deal. This was not only good timing – since Jonathan was well-equipped to negotiate with a company like Lilly, having obtained both a law degree and an MBA from McGill and having studied at the London School of Economics – but it was a curious coincidence. Jonathan had history with Eli Lilly. When he was still in law school he had landed a summer job at Lilly's Scarborough, Ontario, offices. This resulted in his making a valuable contact there, Barry Fishman, but he also got into some trouble, not of his own doing. Here is Jonathan's recollection of his first strange day at the pharmaceutical giant:

I was being shown around the place and I met a woman who, after learning my name, asked me if I happened to be related to Morris Goodman. I said I was. I said he's my father. The next day I was pulled into a VP's office and told they were very concerned with my relationship with Pharmascience. They weren't going to fire me, but they made it clear that I was not permitted to come into the office early, go home late, or work weekends. I was handed over to the head of the diagnostics division who told me she wanted me to write a feasibility study of manufacturing in Canada. To which I said, "Basically, you just want me to do nothing all summer." She didn't say anything, which gave me my answer. That's exactly what she wanted. For this task, this busy work, they gave me a large office in the basement. I called my father and I said, "Look, what they're doing to me." He got angry and told me to quit. "Quit right away," he said. But I couldn't. I'd just gotten myself an apartment and I rode it out till I found a better job, working for Bain and Company, a well-known management-consulting firm. Still, my brief time there was not a complete bust. While I was working at Lilly that summer, Barry Fishman and I became good friends. A few years later, we met again when he was part of the Lilly negotiating team working on the Prozac deal with Pharmascience.

Not surprisingly, sales at Pharmascience doubled during our first year marketing Fluoxetine. As a consequence we began to take on more employees. In a few years, we desperately needed additional space. By the late 1990s, we realized it made more and more sense for Pharmascience's various locations to be centralized in one location. That would happen when we purchased our building at 6111 Royalmount, the one we are still in now.

Again, Jonathan proved to be ideally placed for the job of finding Pharmasicence a suitable home base. In fact, he deserves all the credit for acquiring our current building. He demonstrated great vision in this purchase: in addition to filling a pressing need in our company, the new building turned out to be an amazing deal. Here is Jonathan's recollection of how it came about:

For years, Pharmascience had been located in many different buildings, all within a five-kilometre radius, and it was like we were growing an organ here, another there. There was no cohesiveness. I just thought it made sense to have everything consolidated under one roof, all in one location. I was also looking for an investment. In terms of diversification, it made sense for the family to own real estate. To that end, I started looking all over for a building that would be suitable. It took a while but I finally came across this building owned by the aviation giant Lockheed Martin. This was around the time Jean Chrétien had been re-elected and had decided to kill a very big and prominent helicopter deal for the Canadian military that Lockheed had been awarded by the preceding Mulroney government. For this reason and other financial reasons, Lockheed was highly motivated to sell.

We had an interesting time looking around the place on Royalmount. There are parts of the building that were ... that still are kind of funky. Like the Faraday Shield, for instance: this is best described as a space that's 20,000 square feet and made entirely of lead: that means walls, floor, everything! There is no seal, except for the door. It's especially built to be impervious to spying – from satellites, for instance. Obviously, the kind of thing you are going to need for defence contracts. In fact, the Faraday Shield made me think that Lockheed Martin was going to stay in this building for a long time since it would likely cost hundreds of thousands of dollars just to remove this room. As it happens, this quirk in the building's structure ended up working to our advantage. We negotiated a deal where we bought the building and Lockheed Martin stayed on as a tenant on the top floor. They even threw in all the furniture. What's more, the deal with them was such that if they stayed for the entire length of the lease they would basically be paying for the entire building. Which is exactly what happened: Lockheed's renewed lease ended in 2011.

Despite all this, buying the building was a big expenditure for my father. It also wasn't apparent to him that it was a good investment, not at the beginning. My father is, in many ways, a very cautious man. His philosophy is always to protect his downside. In short, this was a gutsy move for him, but, at the end of the day, my father also has guts. And the decision to move and buy the property on Royalmount paid off: today the building has been expanded twice and is worth multiples more than its original price.

Jonathan always took it for granted he would be involved in the pharmaceutical business. In a profile in his alumni magazine, *McGill News*, Jonathan explained his early attraction to the drug business this way: "Most kids grow up seeing their dads watch sports on TV. My father spent his spare time reading medical periodicals. Instead of having *Sports Illustrated* lying around the house, I'd thumb through copies of the *New England Journal of Medicine*." During his summer breaks from school, Jonathan worked at Pharmascience, taking over the job David had done during his summer breaks – visiting hospital pharmacies and experiencing the challenge of selling to hospital pharmacists. He also worked in the warehouse, made deliveries, and became familiar with the company's operations from the ground floor up.

Still, Jonathan's career path was not always clear or easy. In 1989, he was accepted into the prestigious London School of Economics, which is also when he learned he had Hodgkin's Disease, a form of cancer. He had to leave the LSE and England, returning to Canada for treatment. That was a rough time for him and for all of us. Still, despite his illness, Jonathan never interrupted his studies, earning his BA and graduating, in 1989, with his class at McGill. At that point, he was not sure what path to take. I recommended law. In 1990, he decided on a combined course in law and a Master's of Business Administration and graduated in 1994. While he refused to take the Quebec Bar exam – he did not want to article (known in Quebec as a stage) – he wrote the bar exams in New York and Massachusetts and passed them both.

It should also be noted that in 1999, when Jonathan was making the deal for the building on Royalmount, he was already in the process of running his own pharmaceutical company, Paladin Labs Inc., which was well on its way to becoming a remarkable success story in its own right.

As Jonathan headed out on his own, David continued at Pharmascience and eventually became CEO in 2006. In that role, David has succeeded in transforming the company during a difficult economic period. David has had to deal with the pressure brought to bear on the drug industry by increased government dictates and tighter regulations. The business that I had started in the 1950s has become more challenging, complex, and scientific. Pharmascience has been fortunate to have David in the right place at the right time. His process-oriented mind has proved greatly beneficial in helping the company deal with these new complexities and realities.

In addition to these responsibilities, David has never wavered in his efforts to have Pharmascience make a difference in the community. He has, for instance, orchestrated Pharmascience's annual Centraide drive, which has the company matching donations made by the company's employees. Under David's leadership, Pharmascience has become the largest contributor to Centraide of all pharmaceutical companies in the province of Quebec.

We have also enthusiastically pursued what is now commonly known as pharmaphilanthropy, making it company policy to donate drugs to the underprivileged nations of the world. Since 1995, Pharmascience, working through Health Partners International of Canada (HPIC), has donated approximately $35 million in products to international aid. In 2007, Prime Minister Stephen Harper, attending the opening of the HPIC medical aid distribution centre in Missasssagua, Ontario, commented that "these pallets, stacked with pharmaceutical and medical supplies, represent better health and hope for tens of thousands of children and adults in the developing world."

In 2008, HPIC honoured Pharmascience as the "top donor of medicines," citing our donations of more than $7 million in primary care medicines to its medical aid programs in more than sixty countries. Pharmascience continues to be HPIC's top donor.

Pharmascience has also responded to disasters around the world. In 2004, the tsunami that hit Thailand and other parts of the South Pacific prompted Pharmacience to donate $600,000 in medications. The formal announcement of the donation was made by Mario Deschamps, our recently retired president and general manager of the Pharmascience Group. As Mario pointed out, we have, in addition to the medications, "included pediatric electrolytes to prevent potential dehydration amongst the young." Our employees were also encouraged to make donations, which we matched dollar for dollar.

In 2010, Pharmascience responded to the devastating earthquake in Haiti within twenty-four hours, shipping a wide range of medicines. We also facilitated the desires of our employees to actively participate in the humanitarian relief process. In this case, the catastrophe hit close to home – a number of our 1,400 employees had roots, relatives, and friends in Haiti – and once again we matched the donations our employees made dollar for dollar.

Recently, HPIC president Glen Shepard expressed his gratitude to Pharmascience for its "longstanding commitment to help HPIC improve access to medicine and health care in the developing world."

In the autumn of 1995, I was not feeling well. I met with Ted Wise and we found ourselves seriously discussing our succession plans. Ted's only child, Jeffrey, had graduated from law school and was not interested in the business while David and Jonathan were already working at Pharmascience. We explored a number of options and concluded that Ted would like to exit while I wanted to keep the business for my sons and my family. All it took was a ten-minute conversation between Ted and me to come to an agreement on the price he wanted for his shares. We concluded the sale and purchase of his shares in September of 1995.

Meanwhile, Jonathan was also on his way to take control of Geriatrix, a company listed on the Vancouver Stock Exchange. Geriatrix had been bought by Joddes, which is the Goodman family's holding company. At the suggestion of Jonathan's friend, Mark Piibe, the name Geriatrix was changed to Paladin Inc. At which point, Ted used part of his proceeds from the sale of his share of Pharmascience to invest in Paladin. He became chairman of the board of the fledgling company and remained in that position almost up to his untimely death on 8 August 2013. Jonathan is still proud to point out that Ted made more money from Paladin than he ever did from Pharmascience.

When Jonathan announced he would be leaving Pharmascience in 1995 to start Paladin Labs Inc. with a former colleague, Mark Beaudet, I was not surprised. I understood my son's eagerness to strike out on his own, to make his own way. After all, I had felt the same way when I was his age. "There are many paths up a mountain," I remember telling Jonathan when he told me about his new venture. "And, if those paths get you where you want to go, they're all good." I was also well aware that Jonathan's reasons for starting Paladin were not entirely business-related, as he explains here:

> I am like my father in many respects. First and foremost, I am a control freak and a terrible manager. I am much more interested in building something than in running it. There's a different skill set that goes with being a manager and being an entrepreneur and I am more inclined toward the latter. My father is the same way, which means I knew I couldn't work at Pharmascience be-

cause I couldn't be the boss and, obviously, I wasn't about to replace my father because he is so valuable to the company. Once I
identified that this was my issue at Pharmascience, I knew that I
would have to run my own company, even though I was only
twenty-seven at the time. I told my father my plan, which was
that while Pharmascience was essentially in the generic business,
I intended to focus on the speciality business, specifically a part
of the speciality business my father was running at the time that
was doing about $6 million in sales. But the reps in that business
were old and unmotivated; they were basically lost. So my father
said if I could raise the $6 million from third parties, I could
have the speciality business. That was his condition. My condition was I would raise other people's money and he would have
no say in how the business was run. He said that as long as I
wasn't using his money he couldn't interfere. He never has.

I have always marvelled at Jonathan's business acumen. In part, it
is a consequence of the education he received at McGill and at the
London School of Economics, not to mention his time at Bain. But it
also comes naturally to him. His tenacity, his focus, and his drive are
all an integral part of who he is.

Of course, he is also passionately committed to the art of the deal.
This was obvious with his purchase of our building on Royalmount
Avenue, but perhaps never more obvious than with the start-up of Paladin. Jonathan set about raising the money he needed from three Quebec financial institutions: Royal Bank Capital, Bio Capital, and
Innovatech du Grand Montréal. For our part, Pharmascience invested
our $6 million in products and, as a result, the Goodman family ini-
tially became seventy percent owners of the new company. It is important to mention that his three siblings unanimously supported the
Pharmascience investment in Paladin. Paladin stock was first issued
at $4 a share; now, two decades later, it is trading at over $110 a share.

By any measure, Paladin has been a remarkable success story. It
had revenues of $41,000 in its first year in business; now they exceed
$180 million. According to a recent article in the *Montreal Gazette*,
"Paladin is heading for 16 straight years of record revenue." Along
the way, there has been no shortage of accolades for this new force
in the industry. In 2003, Jonathan and Mark Beaudet were named
Quebec's Entrepreneurs of the Year in the Healthcare/Life Sciences
Field by Ernst & Young. Paladin has also been praised by the

National Post, Profit Magazine, and *Montreal Business Magazine,* among other publications and organizations.

Paladin has succeeded in the way Jonathan intended — by focusing on speciality drugs, by securing Canadian rights to promising new products like Plan B, also known as "the morning after pill." The rights to the controversial Plan B were purchased in 1999. No other company wanted to touch it but Jonathan felt it should be made available to Canadian women. The success of the drug proved that, for Jonathan, too, it is sometimes better to be lucky than to be smart. This seems to be a trait that runs in the Goodman family.

From the start, Jonathan has been a globetrotter in his quest for new products. Early on, that meant flying to just about every country in Europe as well as crisscrossing the United States. He has also gained valuable insights serving, at one time, as one of the fifteen members of the Board of Rx&D Canada, which brings together representatives of Canada's research-based pharmaceutical companies.

I am also proud that Jonathan has found time outside his work at Paladin for community work. For instance, a few years ago, he held a Texas hold'em poker tournament for charity, the first of its kind in Montreal. Paladin has also been the biggest sponsor of the Ride to Conquer Cancer, an annual event for the Segal Centre of the Jewish General Hospital. He has raised donations of over $1.8 million over a three-year period. He has also been involved in Jewish education. Another example of his unique combination of pragmatism and innovativeness was demonstrated in his transformation of ORT's (the Organization of Rehabilitation and Training) annual fundraising concerts at Montreal's Place des Arts. ORT is a worldwide organization that does great work training underprivileged children, but the concert they put on in Montreal never came close to selling out the theatre. Jonathan's idea was to get Montreal's Jewish schools involved in selling tickets and filling the concert hall. His only condition was that the money raised by these schools would go back to the schools in direct proportion to how many tickets they had sold. The result was a full concert hall. In 2012, $1.9 million was raised by the ORT Place des Arts concert, the largest sum ever raised by the organization. Another result of Jonathan's effort was that $1 million went back to Montreal's Jewish schools. Jonathan's vision, his confidence things could be done more effectively, more creatively, was instrumental in making this fundraising effort an unprecedented success.

Along with his commitment to Paladin and to charity, Jonathan has become a dedicated family man. He married Dana Caplan on 28 February 2004 at the Shaar Hashomayim Congregation. Dana has her undergraduate degree from Smith College as well as a law degree from McGill. She has succeeded in grounding Jonathan, giving him a home life that he enjoys tremendously and that helps balance his passionate commitment to his work. We have known Dana since she was a baby as her parents, Mark and Judy Caplan, had a house near ours in Hampstead. Dana is a natural-born mother and together she and Jonathan have three young children, Noah Ezra, Lilah Rose, and Orly Anne (named after Roz's Aunt Anne, her mother's sister). In fact, both my daughters-in-law, Mia and Dana, are wonderful mothers and we could not ask for anything more for our sons. They chose their life-mates well.

Today, I could not be prouder of both my sons' accomplishments in their personal lives as well as in the business world. David has been as solid as a rock in guiding Pharmascience into the twenty-first century. Paladin, meanwhile, continued to grow and reached a market capitalization price of $1.3 billion by the fall of 2013. Then in November 2013, the board of Paladin accepted an offer from the U.S. company Endo Health Solutions Inc. to purchase Paladin. The valuation of Paladin immediately increased to $2.4 billion. Its worth now far exceeds Pharmascience. A phenomenal success story that we are all so proud of.

It is fortunate, as Jonathan says and David echoes, that "there are only two people beyond jealousy – a teacher with his student and a father with his son. We are lucky to have Morris Goodman for both our father and teacher. We have learned so much from his example."

15

Roz

Do not keep yourself apart from the community.
Pirkei Avot

The word for charity does not exist in either Hebrew or Yiddish. That neither language has such a word is hardly a coincidence. Nor is the fact that *tzedakah* is the word that comes closest to what most of us mean by charity. *Tzedekah* can best be defined as righteousness and it is intended to underscore what Jews have always understood about charity – that doing for others is inextricably linked to duty. I learned about this unique notion by example. As a child, growing up with parents who worked incredibly hard just to make ends meet, I watched how my father and mother never failed to fulfill their responsibility to help others. I learned from them that giving to those in need is both a moral and a religious obligation. It is also very gratifying.

But my real education, my graduate course, in *tzedekah* has come, certainly over the last fifty-two years, from seeing my wife, Rosalind, put the practice of philanthropy into action. In a sense, all of us, the whole Goodman family, have been following in Roz's footsteps. For her, *tzedekah* has always been a way of life. Ask anyone in Jewish Montreal about my wife and they will tell you that the name Rosalind Goodman stands for leadership. Her contribution to Montreal's Jewish community has been pervasive and ongoing and has earned her a reputation locally, nationally, and internationally.

Roz's dedication to the community predates me. As a young McGill student she served as a volunteer, then as secretary for Hillel, the international body for Jewish students on university campuses across North America. After we were married, she balanced her responsibilities raising four young children with ever more demanding positions in community organizations. Her growing leadership skills were put to good use by a variety of organizations – starting, as a young married woman, with the Jewish Junior Welfare League and moving on to do volunteer work for the Jewish People's and Peretz Schools and Bialik High School, a school all four of my children attended.

But as Roz would be first to acknowledge, she owes an incalculable debt to the community leaders who preceded her, in particular Dodo Heppner and Milly Lande. I know that Roz still considers Dodo and Milly her mentors. Indeed, it was Dodo and Bernice Brownstein who recruited Roz to head up the Women's Division of the Combined Jewish Appeal (CJA).

But if Roz has managed to make her climb up the ladder of community work look easy – from soliciting for donations to chairing the campaign for the Women's Division of CJA – the truth is it has been the opposite. Not a climb, she will insist, so much as a plunge. Here is her version of events:

I never wanted or expected anything from community work. In large part, I was just following in my mother's footsteps. I got a lot of my love for and faith in this kind of work from her. My memories go back to when I was seven or eight. It was just after the Second World War had ended and the city was filling up with refugees, many of them Holocaust survivors. I remember we adopted a family from Europe, a project initiated by my mother's Hadassah chapter, the Betty Pascal chapter. This meant that we followed and assisted a newly arrived family with a wide variety of things. We would give them advice and help them with information on where to go to obtain whatever services they might need. And I remember my mother taking me to visit this family often. It was a lesson for life — the kind of lesson young people today don't always get from their families, which is what I think they need most of all: an education in seeing what other people go through as well as a sense of ownership in their community. Our generation knew how lucky we were because we were repeatedly told and shown.

I graduated from McGill with the idea that I wanted to be a librarian, but I was married by then and had my first child, Debbie, and all I really wanted to do was stay home with my baby. So when I did get time to do something for myself – it was a privilege then to hire a babysitter; not everyone could – I would spend my time volunteering in the community. It was my way of getting out in the world. I felt like I was doing something useful, something that made a difference. Later, I did a lot of my volunteer work with Debbie, pushing her in the stroller, then with the other children, each in turn.

And as far as the community work went, I was always being offered such nice positions and, in a way, I was always being challenged into accepting them.

In the beginning Roz worked diligently in the background for organizations like the CJA. But she was also, in her own style, a trailblazer. She co-chaired the innovative project of the one-dollar-a-day boxes – reminiscent of the blue Jewish National Fund boxes families like mine had in their homes when I was growing up. Our youngest daughter, Shawna, remembers delivering these boxes, just shoeboxes, which reminded families that giving was easy and also could be routine, a daily obligation. The idea was simple and brilliant: giving just a dollar day added up to something truly substantial by the end of the year.

By 1986, it was becoming increasingly clear that Roz was more than capable of tackling a bigger job. She was offered the job of CJA campaign chair for the Women's Division. But she hesitated:

I remember I was asked to take on the job at Christmas time. I remember, too, that it ruined my holiday. In any case, I asked my kids what I should do. I guess they realized I was trying to find a way out of saying yes and they all said, "Ma, you're a chicken. If it was us you'd tell us it's our responsibility." Still, I came back from that holiday intent on turning down the job. But I was talked into taking it at the last minute. This was very much a turning point and a major challenge for me. That's because I knew that running the campaign meant I would have to speak in public and that had always been a great fear of mine. I was still haunted by an experience I had as a student at McGill. I was taking a fabulous history class, but, after about three weeks, we found out that each of us had to give a lecture. We had to speak to the whole class. I was scared out of my mind. I couldn't speak in public. So I left the class. I always hated myself for that, for running away from a challenge. Later, when I worked in the community, it was always behind-the-scenes. I never wanted the limelight. But taking this job, as campaign chair, meant I had to learn to get over that fear, face that challenge. And I did. I developed slowly: first, by holding cue cards in my hands just so I'd remember my name. My family can tell you about how I would practice my greeting, my opening joke in front of the mirror for days. I always wrote all my own material and I still do. And while it's still hard for me to speak in public, I have learned to do it. Still, I don't take any of it for granted, I don't wing it, but I don't obsess about it like I used to either. I still get nervous, of course, but maybe just on the day of the event, not two weeks in advance.

For me, Roz's fear of speaking out in public and her courage in tackling that fear has always been a measure for me of the strength of her character. The wholehearted commitment she has always shown to me as a wife and partner and as a mother to our children, she has also shown to her community. I would hate to think what my life – or, for that matter, the life of Montreal's community – would be like without her strength and her spirit.

Among Roz's early contributions, in 1986, she introduced to the Montreal Women's Division of CJA the concept of the "Lion of Judah" – a symbolic recognition awarded to women who were major supporters of their local communities. Also, after running the campaign for the Federation CJA Women's Division, Roz accepted another enormous challenge. In 1989, she chaired the Plenary of the Canadian Jewish Congress (CJC) when Dorothy Reitman was CJC president. During her tenure with CJA, she was honoured with the Federation's Outstanding Leadership Award. She co-led, along with Jonathan Wener and Roslyn Wolfe, the 1996 CJA mission to meet Israeli President Shimon Peres. The event brought twelve busloads of Montrealers to Israel. Sadly, the first intifada coincided with this visit and participants were forced to deal with the alarming news that an Israeli public bus had been bombed only two blocks away.

Roz's contribution to the State of Israel also included chairing the Women's Division of Israel Bonds in Montreal as well as co-chairing the whole Montreal Division with the late Mitch Garfinkle. Mitch and his wife, Shirley, became very dear friends of ours. Then Roz had the opportunity to co-chair, along with Roslyn Wolfe, the General

Assembly in Montreal where some 800 North American Jewish Federations were represented, with over 3,500 delegates. It was 1993 and it was a memorable meeting. The late Israeli prime minister Yitzhak Rabin spoke with unmistakable emotion about his experience two months earlier shaking hands with Yassir Arafat on the lawn of the White House. Speaking to a rapt Montreal audience, Prime Minister Rabin candidly recalled: "Of all the hands in the world, [Arafat's] was not the hand I wanted or dreamed of touching. But I was not Yitzhak Rabin on that podium. I stood as the representative of a nation, as the emissary of a nation that wants peace."

One of Roz's most significant roles on behalf of Israel-Montreal cultural exchanges was the part she played in bringing the Dead Sea Scrolls to the city in 2003. This was accomplished with the cooperation of the Israel Museum and Montreal's Pointe à Callière Museum. After the run of the Dead Sea Scroll exhibit (which attracted capacity crowds throughout its engagement), Roz became co-chair with Karys Marcus of the Canadian Friends of the Israel Museum in Montreal.

And Roz kept finding new roles to play in the community – for instance, she was co-founder with Roslyn Wolfe and Elaine Goldstein of Mazon Food Fest. Mazon, founded by DoDo Heppner, is an organization that concentrates on the Jewish response to hunger in the world and the funds raised in this particular event were distributed to food banks across the province.

Then in 2005, there was the Tel Aviv University's "Visas for Life Exhibition," which Roz organized with Sue Carol Isaacson. The exhibit, which was displayed at the University of Montreal and at the park opposite Montreal's City Hall, honoured 100 diplomats who had served in Nazi-occupied countries during the Second World War and who had risked their careers, and often their lives, to save men, women, and children, many of them Jews, in peril.

One of the most moving stories chronicled in the exhibit was that of Aristides de Sousa Mendes, who was Portugal's consul-general in Marseilles during the war. During his tenure, the Portuguese government gave him strict instructions to adhere to the orders of France's Vichy government, a body dominated by Nazi sympathizers and collaborators. These orders, as a consequence, were inhumane and clearly anti-Semitic. He was permitted to issue only rare visas for occasional refugees seeking entry to neutral Portugal and, of course, none were to be offered to Jewish refugees. However, when a rabbi sought help from Mendes, he was prepared to risk making an exception and process visas for the rabbi and his family. The rabbi had a condition, however. He said, "Help not only me, but the others in danger. Help them all." The Portuguese diplomat recognized his responsibility to his fellow human beings in dire need and responded by working, along with his wife and children, around the clock to issue thousands of visas – saving many who ended up crossing the Pyrenees to Spain and were then able to go on to Lisbon, the only port on the Atlantic not under Nazi control. (The personal connection here is worth repeating – Mendes helped my friend Thomas Hecht and his family escape the Nazis and find refuge in Canada.) Eventually, the Portuguese government recalled Mendes and stripped him of his wealth and title. After the war, he survived with food provided by a Jewish soup kitchen. He died in 1954. Incidentally, his wife and two children eventually moved to Quebec. It would be many years before Mendes's story was told in full, in exhibits like the one Roz helped bring to Montreal. Today, his name is inscribed in Yad Vashem as "a righteous gentile" and his story stands as a shining example of the Jewish tradition of tzedekah. Proof, too, that you do not have to be Jewish to practice the tradition.

These are just a few examples from Roz's more than half-century of dedication to and hard work on behalf of Montreal's Jewish community. I could not be prouder of her. I also take as much pleasure as she does whenever we cross the border into the United States and the question is asked of her by some inquisitive border guard, "What do you do for a living?" Roz invariably replies, "I am a professional volunteer." Invariably, the guard just stares at her.

◆

The contribution Roz has made to the community demonstrates that philanthropy can, indeed, be a full-time job. So while I have always supported my wife's philanthropic efforts and have, as a consequence, attended more than my share of chicken dinners and galas, I have spent the vast majority of my time with my head buried in my work, focused, certainly in the last three decades, on growing Pharmascience. Still, I can trace the exact moment I lifted my head up to one fateful day, almost ten years ago. That was the day Dr. Jacques Turgeon, the dean of the Faculty of Pharmacy at the University of Montreal, my alma mater, surprised me by showing up at my office to make a request. We were both busy men so he skipped the formalities. He got right to the point.

"Morris, we're looking for someone to fund an Agora at the university. This structure will serve as a meeting place and study hall for University of Montreal pharmacy students," Jacques explained. He went on to show me pictures of what he expected the Agora would look like. The plan was to situate the meeting place between the Marcelle Coutu IRIC Building and the Jean Coutu Faculty of Pharmacy Building. Agora, incidentally, is the Greek word for marketplace and, in the context of a university setting, it would serve, appropriately enough, as a genuine marketplace of ideas. Jacques also went on to detail what the U of M was going to require from me by way of financial support. But to be honest, the whole time he was talking, I found myself struggling to wrap my head around the request that was suddenly and unexpectedly being made of me – me, I could not help thinking, of all people.

"Why are you asking me?" I finally said, still a little bewildered by the improbable conversation we appeared to be having.

"The answer to that is simple, Morris; it's because you're successful. You are very successful," he said.

"I am? Are you sure? Because I don't really think I am." In retrospect, I can see how odd this statement must have sounded to Jacques. Except I meant every word I was saying. I was not kidding and I was not being unduly modest. The fact is I do not think, until that moment, I ever realized what my confrères in the pharmaceutical industry thought of me, how, as Jacques explained, people were looking to me to lead by example.

"You may not realize it," he said, "but your colleagues are watching how your business is growing; they're aware of everything that has been accomplished at Pharmascience."

Jacques had woken me up to a reality I had until that moment been curiously unaware of. Perhaps because I was working so hard to make Pharmascience a success, I never took the time to measure that success. I told Dr. Turgeon, in Roz's presence, since she just happened to be at the office that day, that I would have to think about his request. When we got home, Roz's matter-of-fact response was immediate and exactly what I would have expected of her. "You have the money," she said. "Why wouldn't you do it?"

Perhaps because of her own work as a fundraiser and, more likely, because we have been married a long time, Roz understands the complicated relationship I have with philanthropy. She also understood that the meeting with Jacques Turgeon was a turning point for me.

As she puts it:

> You have to understand Morris's psychology of giving. The
> thought of going backwards is his biggest nightmare. He has that
> immigrant family's mentality that makes him never want to give
> too much one year because he would then worry what if he
> couldn't honour his pledge the next year. We have a lot of friends
> who do well and when they have a big year they donate substan-
> tially. But if the next year is a bad one, then they cut back. This
> was not acceptable to Morris. He is determined to honour his
> commitments and so he proceeds slowly. But that meeting with
> Jacques Turgeon was big time. With the Agora, Morris didn't
> proceed slowly. He really plunged.

Roz is right. I have been cautious. I guess I still recall Rabbi Bender's
words from when I was a boy about the coin being round and rolling
from one person to another. Still, from the moment we made the decision
to say yes to the Agora, both Roz and I were convinced we had done
the right thing. The commitment to the Morris and Rosalind Goodman
Agora was signed in February 2003 and it officially opened in 2005. The
Agora has proven to be an enormously successful location for a variety
of university functions. In fact, it is the most popular gathering place on
the campus. To that date, it was far and away our family's largest gift.

But it would not be our last. In 2007, Roz and I were also honoured
by Montreal's Jewish Public Library (JPL) – which will celebrate its one
hundredth anniversary in 2014, making it the oldest Jewish library in
North America – with a gala, hosted by CBC television personality Rick
Mercer. A Goodman gift to the JPL created the Rosalind and Morris
Goodman Family Heritage and Digital Preservation Centre in the JPL's
archives.

Through the years Roz and I have contributed to Hope and Cope,
the support service for cancer patients originated at Montreal's Jewish
General Hospital by Sheila Kussner, herself a cancer survivor and an
inspirational leader. In 2006, Roz agreed to co-chair an extravaganza
celebrating the twenty-fifth anniversary of the Hope and Cope program. As it happened, a year later, Roz was diagnosed with lung cancer
and began a treatment program during which she experienced and was
appreciative of the services provided by the Hope and Cope volunteers.
A year after that, we were the honourees of Hope and Cope's Fashion
Fantasy XVIII.

In December 2006, our family made a transformative gift to the Jewish General Hospital to establish the hospital's Comprehensive Stroke Centre. The Stroke Centre's work has already shown significant results with its participation in a national study on "stroke outcome in those over 80." The team was led by the then-chief of neurology, Dr. Calvin Melmed, my son David's father-in-law. The study analyzed nearly 27,000 patients with ischemic stroke, also known as mini-strokes. These patients were admitted to some 600 hospitals across Canada and, as a consequence of following this group, the authors came up with strategies that should be implemented "to facilitate equal access to specialized stroke care for the elderly." Another improvement that Calvin made to the Comprehensive Stroke Centre with our donation was to recruit Dr. Alexander Thiel to the department as a research neurologist.

Then in 2008, we were approached by Dr. Richard Levin, dean of the McGill Medical School, about making another "big time" contribution, this time to McGill University, Roz's alma mater. Dean Levin was asking us to get involved in the University's Cancer Research Centre. We heard him out but we also wanted to see the Centre for ourselves. So one day, after we had been at the gym, we dropped in on the director, Dr. Michel Tremblay, completely unannounced. He was in the middle of a meeting and it was clear he had no idea who we were. We introduced ourselves and said that we just came by to see "what you guys do around here." Michel would confess later that he thought we were lost and had wandered into the Centre to use the washroom. After he showed us around, though, we knew we were going to contribute to the Centre and provide him with funds for the building as well as for a chair in lung cancer research. The agreement with McGill University was signed in September 2008.

Our donation was transformative and, as a result of it, the Cancer Research Centre was renamed the Rosalind and Morris Goodman Cancer Research Centre. This new Goodman facility ties together two new research programs – those conducted by the McGill Cancer Research Centre and by the Molecular Oncology Group of the McGill University Health Centre (MUHC). Our Centre is also part of the University's new Bellini Life Sciences Complex – created from a donation from Dr. Francesco Bellini. The Complex houses 600 scientists working together in bio-medical, developmental biology, and cancer research. Thus far, McGill researchers have made significant contributions in the fight against cancer, starting in 1967 when Dr. Phil Gold, then twenty-nine, discovered Carcinoembryonic antigen (CEA), the marker for colon cancer. More recently, there was the discovery of the PTP1B gene, associated with the propagation of breast cancer in two of five affected women. McGill University researchers have also identified the gene that causes spina bifida.

It has not just been the researchers who are thinking big, though. When it comes to philanthropy, Roz has proved particularly talented at generating big ideas. In 2010, a brainstorming session led Roz to organize "a larger-than-life gala" in support of the Rosalind and Morris Goodman Cancer Research Centre (GCRC). The inaugural gala – the first of its kind at McGill – was a huge success, raising $2.5 million. Then in 2012, a follow-up exceeded everyone's expectations. The plan, as it stands now, is to continue the gala bi-annually. Roz is currently at work on a cookbook that promises to raise additional funds for the Goodman Cancer Research Centre. With projects like this, Roz has also set out to address the fact that McGill's Cancer Centre has gone mainly unnoticed by the public. She is determined to not only make the Centre a force in the scientific world, which to some degree it already is, but a much better known force, one that will be sure to attract brilliant students interested in research.

During her own battle with lung cancer, Roz has displayed tremendous courage in dealing with the psychological toll that such a diagnosis can take on a person. But she has never been deterred from continuing her outreach to the community and especially to the Goodman Cancer Research Centre. If anything, it has made her work harder raising funds for the Centre.

In time, I am convinced Roz's work with the Centre will prove to be substantially more significant than any financial donation we have made. For one thing, raising the Centre's profile will build a fundraising infrastructure that will continue to acquire the best equipment and continue to attract the best minds. Roz also started a free lecture series, which is open to the general public. It has become an increasingly well-attended event. As far as we are concerned, the driving force behind the success of the lecture series comes from our understanding that knowledge is power, particularly when a person is facing serious health problems. We are aware that in at least one instance the knowledge acquired at a lecture series saved the life of a friend.

In 2011, McGill awarded both Roz and me honorary LLD's for our philanthropic efforts. In retrospect, our major philanthropic acts over the last decade, whether it was building the Agora at the University of Montreal or the Rosalind and Morris Goodman Cancer Research Centre at McGill University, have proven to be an extraordinary opportunity as well as a great privilege for Pharmascience and, most of all, for me and my family.

Philanthropy has also provided me with an opportunity to understand the significance of being part of something larger than one's self and the significance of contributing to a community. On 18 September 2008, I had the chance to give a speech at the dedication of the Rosalind and Morris Goodman Cancer Centre and to reflect on how much giving to others had, in turn, given to me.

> Some 1,800 years ago, during the first stage of the Talmudic period, the Sages of Judaism assembled a body of literature known as the *Pirkei Avot – Ethics of Our Fathers*. In this body of work, the Rabbis outlined a path to lead a moral and just life. The precepts that they laid down in the first few centuries of the Common Era have become the basis for the moral code that permeates Western society. Standing before you here today, I would like to share with you one particular passage from this body of work that has always inspired me.

> > Do not keep yourself apart from the community. Let your home be a gathering place for wise men, sit attentively at their feet, and drink of their words and wisdom with eagerness. Where there is no knowledge, there is no understanding; where there is no understanding, there is no knowledge.

> Rosalind and I and the rest of the Goodman family realize the importance of giving back to the community and it is our hope that this cancer research centre will be a model for the principles that the sages had in mind.

> I also made a point of recognizing in my speech on that special day that whatever contribution our family was making to the Goodman Cancer Research Centre would be carried forward by the men and women who would persevere in looking for effective treatments, even cures.

We all know that a house is comprised of bricks and mortar. It is only when you add a family, ethical values, and a soul that it becomes a home. It is Rosalind's and my wish that this centre becomes imbued with the knowledge of the educators, researchers, and students who will inhabit its physical confines. Through your work we hope that you will breathe life into the walls and transform it into a home – a home that will become a significant contributor to further our understanding and to find the causes, the treatments, and the cures that the world longs for.

Finally, it was especially moving to have our Centre sharing a space with a building – The Bellini Life Sciences Complex – named in honour of the renowned Italian-Canadian Francesco Bellini, who famously brought the first anti-AIDs drug to market based on research done at McGill. His was a miraculous discovery, one that has made a life-changing difference in the lives of countless people as it proved to be instrumental in turning AIDs, a disease once viewed as a death sentence, into what it so often is today: a manageable chronic disease. I concluded my speech with an expression of my lifelong gratitude to my country on my behalf as well as Roz's and my family's and on behalf of Dr. Bellini. "Thank you, Canada," I said, "for allowing this immigrant, Francesco Bellini, and the son of an immigrant, Morris Goodman, to be able to reach this milestone."

16

Pulling Together

You must do the thing you think you cannot do.
Eleanor Roosevelt.

Writing this book has served to remind me how a life can change forever in a day. Take, for instance, the day I walked into Manny Winrow's neighbourhood drugstore and asked for a job as a delivery boy, or the day I decided to go into business for myself, which marked the founding of Winley-Morris, or the day I sold that business, or that day, more than fifty-two years ago now, that I met a charming young woman named Rosalind Druker. In each of these cases, my path seemed set for me. Some days, though, the path is not nearly as clear; it is, indeed, far darker and much harder to navigate. 17 August 2011 was such a day.

It was a clear, sunny Wednesday afternoon, three o'clock, when I received a call from Dana, my son Jonathan's wife. She was crying, struggling to get the words out. She told me that Jonathan had been cycling in the Laurentians with his staff at Paladin, celebrating the closure of a business deal. The ride was the kind of the thing Jonathan did regularly and expertly. But this time something had gone wrong – there had been an accident, a bad one. Dana explained that Jonathan's friend and vice-president at Paladin, Mark Beaudet, had called to tell her that Jonathan had fallen from his bicycle. No one had been around him when the accident occurred. All we knew was that Jonathan was unconscious.

It occurs to me now that what I just said about a life changing in a day needs to be amended. A life changes in an instant. Before that phone call, I had been busy in my office at Pharmascience, working

on something I am sure I considered important at the time, something presumably urgent that needed to get done; after Dana's call,
everything I had been doing before, everything I considered important or necessary, suddenly no longer mattered. None of it; it all left
my head, immediately. My life, the life of my family, and most of
all, the life of my son and his wife and children, were compromised,
hanging in the balance. And it all happened in an instant, a split-
second.

Indeed, a split second later, there were new, truly urgent decisions
to make. A new reality had set in just like that. Dana wanted to
know where the ambulance should take Jonathan. I knew there were
only two trauma centres in the city – Montreal General and Sacré-
Coeur, in the northeast sector of the city. Sacré-Coeur was chosen
because it was closer. Meanwhile, Dana's mother, Judy Caplan, had
rushed over to Dana's house to be with her and to take care of Dana
and Jonathan's young children, Noah, Lilah, and Orly. I told Dana
that I would be right over to pick her up. The plan, insofar as we
had one, was for Dana and me to drive to the hospital together.

What happened next remains a blur. What was I thinking as I
drove to my son's house? What was I thinking as Dana and I made
our way to the hospital? What was said? I have no memory of any
of it. The next thing I remember is that we arrived at the Sacré-Coeur
Trauma Centre and we waited in the hallway for Jonathan to arrive
in an ambulance. After waiting awhile, Dana and I were escorted
into a room and we saw Jonathan unconscious, connected to all
sorts of life-support and breathing equipment. Dana remembers
thinking he looked relaxed, as if he might be taking a nap. But a doctor eventually came out to see us and told us Jonathan had suffered
an extremely serious head injury. He was in a coma.

Obviously, those first days were critical. So much so I did not want
to believe just how critical they were. The first thing I did after the
accident was call Guy Breton, the rector of the University of
Montreal, to make sure Jonathan had the best doctor available. He
was reassuring. Sacré-Coeur is part of the University of Montreal's
teaching network and it is the trauma centre for all points north
of Montreal.

Our family came together to rally to Jonathan's side. My message
to everyone could not have been simpler. "He is going to come out
of this," I told everyone and, no doubt, myself, "and he's going to
come out perfect."

And while there was not a lot of evidence to base my opinion on, I clung to it steadfastly. In retrospect, I think I instinctively believed that if I did not, I would spiral into a depression. My children will tell you that I am the worrier in the family, but during this critical time I was doing my best to keep the worry at bay. For her part, Roz was typically strong and set the tone for our family with her mantra: "Where there is life, there is hope."

Of course, you cling to whatever scrap of faith or hope you can during such times and one hopeful early sign was given by Calvin Melmed, David's father-in-law. It turns out there are advantages to having a former chief of neurology in the family. When Jonathan arrived at the trauma centre, there was initial concern that he was unable to move his right side. Fear of paralysis was one more fear to add to all the others. But, according to Calvin, Jonathan did have some feeling in his extremities. Calvin squeezed Jonathan's toes the night of the accident and there was a reaction, a small but enormously reassuring reaction. Calvin could say this much at least: he believed that whatever paralysis Jonathan had suffered, there was a chance it might not be permanent. He had some sensation. Calvin provided us with our first small but significant ray of hope.

Every Sunday Calvin would show up at Sacré-Coeur, take out his medical kit, and examine Jonathan. For his diligence, we will be eternally grateful! We are also grateful to the dedicated doctors at Sacré-Coeur who treated Jonathan, including Yoan Lamarche, Yanick Beaulieu, Martin Albert, Patrick Bellemare, Soasig Leguillan, and Paul Khoueir.

Calvin had also contacted Dr. Michael Seidel, a former student of his who was practising at the Sacré-Coeur at the time, and Dr. Seidel did his best to keep us as up to date as possible. He would come around every day to talk to us, though all he could say was, "It's serious." His face seemed set in stone when he delivered this news or, more precisely, this absence of news. But it was clear he was not going to soften the situation. All the doctors we spoke to at the Sacré-Coeur were equally cautious. There were also some who were undeniably pessimistic. More than once, my family and I were told that it would take a miracle for Jonathan to recover.

The diagnosis Jonathan had been given when he first came in was "diffused axonal injury." Loosely defined, this means that there is no one particular spot in the brain that is affected by the injury. In effect, the whole brain has moved in the skull. As a result, the neurons all have to reconnect on their own and there is really nothing to do but wait to see if, and how effectively, this occurs. Concern about the pressure on his brain was a constant in the early days after the accident and the surgical neurosurgeon, Dr. Khoueir, drilled holes in Jonathan's skull to relieve the pressure.

Meanwhile, Dana told her children that their daddy was sleeping in the hospital and being treated by a very good team of doctors. The children continued to ask about their father and Dana kept repeating the same explanation. The children would not see Jonathan until he regained consciousness and was able to speak.

August 26th was a very critical and difficult day. Jonathan suffered two serious complications as a further result of the fall. He developed a thrombosis in his leg, which travelled to his lung, causing cardiac fibrillation. In other words, he suffered a small heart attack. At the same time, he developed a pulmonary embolism.

Jonathan remained in a coma for a week, then two; it was a terrible time. I recall Dana and Shawna talking to him constantly, telling him about their daily activities, about the kids, about going shopping, anything in the hope he might be listening. Mia, David's wife, visited Jonathan every morning at eight and would phone Roz to report on his condition.

For Dana, life had to carry on. Despite all the pressure on her, she kept up the nursing of her baby, Orly, who was ten months old, and took care of her other two children, Lilah, who was four, and Noah, who was six. At night, Dana would return home from the hospital, put the kids to bed, and then return to the hospital. Her mother held down the fort at Dana and Jonathan's home, moving in with her for a week, and Dana's father, Mark Caplan, took on the role of chauffeur; he insisted on driving his daughter to and from the hospital several times a day.

Dana was especially nervous about how Noah, who was starting grade two at Akiva School, and Lilah, who was at the Foundation School, would deal with going back to school and how the other children would treat them. The schools sent out an email to the other parents to explain what had happened to Jonathan, asking them to be respectful of the family's privacy. This proved to be a great support for Dana. Support also came from Judy's sisters, Robin and Susan, who took turns helping out at their niece's house.

During Jonathan's stay in Sacré-Coeur, we became friends with the
family of Jean-Marc Dupuis, who had fallen off his second story bal-
cony and landed on his head. His accident had occurred a day earlier
than Jonathan's and he was in a coma in the next room. It was helpful
to be able to discuss Jonathan's progress with another family going
through the same sort of life-threatening experience. As a result, a
strong bond was formed between us and the Dupuis family. Later,
when both Jonathan and Jean-Marc recovered, the doctors would
cite the cases as two miracles in one week.

In the meantime, the news of the accident hit Montreal's business
community hard as Paladin was a successful, publicly traded company on the Toronto Stock Exchange. The Jewish community was
also reeling. I remember Rabbi Shuchat, rabbi emeritus of our synagogue, the Shaar Hashomayim, calling to tell me the whole city was
worried about Jonathan. Indeed, given the reach of Paladin as well
as Pharmascience, the whole world seemed to be touched by this
freak accident. People were contacting us from Jerusalem to Vietnam.
Two of Jonathan's friends, Gideon Pollack and Jeffrey Hart, came to
the hospital every evening to read to him. Another friend, David
Zeman, flew in from Singapore to see him. Milan Panic, found out
what had happened from his stepson and he called me soon after the
accident. He made it a point to call me every week while Jonathan
was in the hospital. We never talked business. We talked, instead,
about our families. His efforts to reach out to me in this situation
were especially moving. Even more moving was the fact that he kept
calling regularly, every week, to find out if there was any progress. It
was a heartfelt gesture that continues to mean a lot to me.

After the accident, Roz began to keep a journal. In it, she provides
a poignant chronicle of how trying this time was for her, for all of us.
The first page bears the date – August 17th – and this chilling impromptu title: "Jonathan's Terrible Bike Accident." Two weeks later,
Roz wrote: "The hardest part of the day is just getting out of bed to
face the day with hope."

As it turns out, Roz's journal proved to be a day-to-day record of
hope. Throughout it, she wrote down quotes for reassurance and sol-
ace – like Eleanor Roosevelt's remark about the necessity of doing
that thing you think you cannot do. Tellingly, though, the first quote
she wrote in the journal was about the nature of true friendship. It
was written by the actress Marlene Dietrich, who said, "It's the
friends you can call up at four who matter." And we were fortunate

to have many friends like that in our life. Indeed, Roz's journal chron-
icles, along with our concern for Jonathan's progress, all the people
who supported our family, doing small things, cooking, picking people up at the airport, keeping us company, pulling together, day after
day, night after night. Roz relates, for instance, how on "Day 3"
Abby Scheier, the wife of Shaar Hashamayim's Rabbi Adam Scheier,
organized a woman's circle at her home. As Roz wrote in her journal
at the time:

> We gathered to bake challahs and say psalms ... Everyone there
> had a connection to Jonathan. It was so beautiful to connect
> with each other and to be able to feel everyone's love and sup-
> port. Jonathan is so loved + appreciated.

In my case, Ronald Reuben dropped by the hospital regularly. I
know he had been enlisted by my family to keep me distracted, to talk
business during those long hours and days in the waiting room.
Ronald did his job well. He was, in my daughter Debbie's words, "a
godsend."

A voice from the more distant past also came in the person of Edward Pantzer, calling from New York City. He was the son of Myron
Pantzer, founder of Panray. Myron had been one of my first suppliers
and one of my early mentors in the business when I was starting out
in the pharmaceutical business in the early 1950s. Winley-Morris's
association with Panray, in particular our distribution of its tuberculosis treatment Parasal INH, had been a turning point for my young
company back then. Now, Myron's son Edward was calling because
he had heard about Jonathan's accident from associates in New York.
He immediately offered to send his private jet, his helicopter, whatever was required, to transport Jonathan to New York.

"He should be in New York," he told me. But while I appreciated
the generosity of the offer, I told him we were not thinking of moving
Jonathan yet. "We have good doctors, good specialists, too," I
pointed out. But he was persistent. He told me that Robin Solomon,
a top administrator at New York's Mt. Sinai Hospital, would call me.
Robin, he added, had contacts throughout the city and could put me
in touch with the top trauma specialists in New York. And she did
call, right away. She told me we should consider taking Jonathan to
see Dr. Jamshid Ghajar, renowned chief of trauma at the Brain
Trauma Foundation, located at the Rockefeller Center. This was just

a week after the accident, but when I spoke to Dr. Ghajar, he told me frankly that there was no point in bringing Jonathan to him. "I can't do anything for your son now. I'm really only good in the first week," he said. But he also said something that would prove to be remarkably prescient and reassuring. "Mr. Goodman," he said, "I'll give you one piece of advice: don't listen to anyone for six months. No one knows what is going to happen."

This reinforced what we had already been hearing from Calvin Melmed. Still, it was important for us to hear it stated again. It gave us the energy to keep saying that Jonathan would recover, despite the pessimism of some of the doctors. On Day 15 – August 31st, according to Roz's journal, Jonathan's eyes opened for the first time, although he did not have control of them. They were darting all around. Soon, that changed to a blank stare. But three days later, the eighteenth day after the accident, he recognized us. He was partially out of the coma, making significant progress. It was enough for us to believe that the long road back was starting, a road that would have a lot of difficult twists and turns and would still, for many days to come, have us asking ourselves the question, "What state will he be in?"

◆

"It teaches you that bad news is just a phone call away," my youngest daughter, Shawna, now says. She recalls the aftermath of her brother's accident this way:

> You adjust to a new reality. You move forward. I can also say that no one in my family ever hid under a blanket. They faced what had happened, right away. It was horrible as horrible could be, but it was faced ... My father's strength was to make it clear that we were a team. We all took a role in what was happening. I remember I kept saying to myself, "Thank God, I am part of a family, part of this family." I had no clue how someone would handle all this alone. It would simply be too much.

Shawna is the youngest in the family, the baby, the one we all doted on. In addition to Roz and me, she had her three siblings to pay constant attention to her. And because she was closest in age to Jonathan – Jonathan is four years older – the relationship between the two has always been especially close. To this day, Jonathan likes to claim that he raised Shawna.

But it was clear from the beginning that Shawna was born with her own uniquely outgoing personality. I can still remember early mornings, peeking into her room before I went to work, and seeing the sun slanting across her crib as she woke up, happy, always happy. Mostly, though, I remember she woke up singing. This kind of talent for joy and for sharing is a gift very few people are given in life. To this day, singing with my youngest, Shawna, is one of my great joys in life.

Shawna married on 20 October 1996. Her husband, Todd Sone, son of Gersh and Sheila Sone, is a Torontonian. He has a BA from the University of Toronto and an MBA from the Wharton School of Business. He and Shawna met at Camp Ramah in Utterson, Ontario, when they were both eighteen, and have been together almost ever since. As a matter of fact, I knew Todd's father, Gersh, forty years ago; he is a pharmacist in Toronto and I had done business with him. Todd now works for the New York–based health care fund Signet and commutes from Montreal to New York City. Together, Shawna and he have three wonderful sons: Zachary, thirteen, Andrew, ten, and Nathaniel, seven. Their children all attend private Jewish school and are all typically happy boys. All three love sports. Shawna and Todd are active in the Jewish community and make a great team. With their children, they lead a traditional Jewish life.

Shawna remains a people-person. She has always had a knack for making others feel included. One of the ways she has continued to do this is through her love of cooking and, in particular, teaching cooking. After studying at the Cordon Bleu Institute in Paris, she studied to be a pastry chef in New York. Back in Montreal, she has taught public classes in cooking at places like Loblaw's and at Jewish organizations like Hadassah and the National Council of Jewish Women. Currently, she is succeeding at a new venture – offering housekeepers a series of classes, which are paid for by their employers. It is an original idea she and her mother came up with and, thus far, it is proving to be very successful.

Shawna also used her knowledge of cuisine to compile the 2005 cookbook *Panache: Montreal's Flare for Kosher Cooking*. When this elegant and pragmatic book came out the reviews were glowing, including this rave from prolific Canadian cookbook author Rose Reisman:

Panache has an eclectic range of outstanding recipes. The bonus is that they are all kosher. I have read virtually all of the kosher cookbooks on the shelves today and none can compare to the creativity of *Panache*.

Panache was conceived as a fundraising project with the Women's Auxiliary of the Jewish General Hospital and has so far gone through three printings and raised nearly $200,000 for the hospital.

Shawna acquire her taste for community work from her mother early on – starting with those CJA dollar-a-day shoeboxes she delivered for Roz – and she has gone on to serve as the chair for the CJA's young leadership campaign. During her tenure she has spearheaded projects like "Cooking for a Cause" and "Soup for Shut-ins." She has also organized after-school cooking programs. Her goal in all these endeavours has been to look for tangible projects that people can handle with relative ease but that also give them a true sense of accomplishment. Shawna traces her own commitment to fundraising back to growing up in a busy, involved house:

> There was always some project in the works at our house. I remember once my mother was organizing a fashion show for the synagogue and the house was full of perfume samples we were going to give away at the event. Instead, I filled up my schoolbag with the samples and went up and down our street selling them door-to-door.

As for me, I like to think I instilled in Shawna the importance of a good education and of choosing an occupation you enjoy doing. Here is how she puts it:

> Find something you love and you will never have to work a day in your life is what my father always told us – my sister and brothers and me. Find your focus and stick to it. It didn't matter to him what that focus was. All that mattered was you were absorbed in it one hundred percent. Because of my father, I am still always thinking: "What are my priorities? What should I be focusing on next?"

The quality I admire most in my eldest daughter, Debbie, is her capacity to always be there when you need her, this despite the fact that she, of all my children, chose early on to make her life outside Montreal. After Jonathan's accident, Debbie returned to Montreal for long stretches and, in a way, it felt like she had never left. During those long days and nights immediately after the accident, when I was trying my best to remain optimistic, it was Debbie to whom I would confide, "This is hard, so hard."

Debbie, as the eldest, has always had my number. For instance, she knows I am the worrier in the family. In fact, she loves to recall the time seven years ago when we were all in Israel for her daughter Lizzie's bat mitzvah and I went a little crazy. Here is her accurate version of events and of my behaviour:

Most of the family had come for the bat mitzvah and a handful of us decided to walk to the Wailing Wall one Shabbat evening. My mother was there, my father, my husband, his brother, and his brother's wife. On the way back, I guess my sister-in-law and I must have gotten engrossed in a conversation and we just kept walking back to the hotel, thinking everyone else was right behind us. But they weren't. So we assumed they had gone back to the hotel on their own. But they weren't there either. I immediately started to worry about my father. I knew they were going to be looking for us and he was going to be panicking. I remember my sister-in-law didn't think anything of it, but then she doesn't know my father like I do.

Later, I found out what had happened. When my father noticed we were missing, he dragged everyone in the group to a police station. The Israeli police asked, "How long has your daughter been gone?" He said, "Ten minutes." Then they asked, "How old is she?" And he said, "She's forty-two." They kicked him out of the station.

Jonathan's accident also reinforced for Debbie, as it did for all of us, the value of a big family and the support they and, in turn, the people around them provide. "The doctors kept telling us it was going to take a miracle for Jonathan to get better," Debbie has since said, "but, as a family, we hung on to that."

Debbie, perhaps because she was the eldest, felt more compelled than her siblings to carve out her own path. She left home at seventeen, in part because, as she told me, she felt stifled being with the same set of students she had been with from nursery school through CEGEP at Marianopolis. Her decision was one neither Roz nor I were happy about, but we ended up making a deal with her. If she could get into an Ivy League School in the United States, she could go. And she got into Cornell, choosing art history as her major. Those museums her mother was always taking her to when she was a little girl were clearly an inspiration to her. She went on to get her Master's degree in art history at the University of Chicago.

Today, Debbie lives in Manhattan with her husband, Gerald (Gerry) Davis, the son of Mariam Davis and the late John Davis. Debbie and Gerry met at Cornell University, where he went on to study architecture. He also received a Master's degree in real estate from New York University and an MBA from Columbia. While he worked as a banker for a time, he eventually returned to his first love, working as an architect, developing and building condominiums. Debbie and Gerry were married on 29 August 1991. They are a wonderful couple as well as devoted parents to their daughter, Elizabeth (Lizzie), and their son, Ben. Elizabeth, named after my late mother-in-law Edith Doner Levenson, is a sophmore today at Brown University. Ben attends Heschel High School in New York City. He likes science but at the moment is passionate about competitive swimming and is excellent at it.

While Debbie, as the big sister, is very close to Shawna, the two of them are also very different. Where Shawna is outgoing, Debbie is reserved. She is also a bookworm, the intellectual in the family. And while it has taken her some time to establish her desired career in the arts, she has accomplished that in the last six years, giving art tours of museums and galleries, and putting out a monthly newsletter in which she analyzes affordable works of art for her subscribers. She is currently working as an art advisor, helping people develop their art collections. Along the same lines, she has also been building a photography collection for Pharmascience. Her most recent project is a children's book she wrote called *Speeding Down the Spiral: An Artful Adventure*, set in New York City's famous Guggenheim Museum. It came out in the fall of 2012, launched at an art gallery in Chelsea.

Debbie remains a wonderful daughter, who has a strong sense of family and has also taught me to see the world differently. I acknowledge that I still do not always see in a work of art what she or, for that matter, her mother sees, but I have learned a lot from her. My children, Debbie in particular, have introduced me to new and different perspectives of the world.

◆

Perhaps the most important thing about being a parent is acknowledging the path of each of your children, recognizing each child's uniqueness. For Roz and me, all that mattered was that our children did the best they could and did what they loved to do. So while I have never wavered from my decision to maintain Pharmascience as

a family business, I have also never regretted the fact that it was not
a business either of my daughters was drawn to. Shawna worked for
the company for a few summers while she was in school and Debbie
did a longer stint with Pharmascience when her children were young
because the job enabled her to work from home, but in both cases
it was not a job either one felt attached to. This never bothered me.
In fact, it was obvious that the pharmaceutical business was not for
them. What's more, I am sure I would have felt the same way if
David and Jonathan had not been drawn to the pharmaceutical business, but, of course, that was not the case. Both were destined to
join me in my line of work and I knew this early on. I also cannot
deny I have derived a great deal of pride and pleasure – in Yiddish,
the word that perfectly combines both feelings is *nachas*— in working with my sons.

Even so, it has sometimes been complicated for David and
Jonathan to work together. As boys, close in age, they have occasionally had problems getting along. David has a good mind, but he
sometimes solves problems differently than his brother. He is more
methodical, cautious, less direct. Jonathan is the opposite and has
not always been patient with David. This aspect of their relationship
was often exacerbated when they were both employed at Pharmascience. When Jonathan decided to start Paladin, David found his
brother's move surprising and difficult to accept. I inevitably found
myself stuck in the middle, watching as their lifelong family dynamic
played out in front of me. Jonathan was convinced we could not all
work together at Pharmascience and made his decision about Paladin accordingly; meanwhile, David did not understand why it was
necessary for things to change. Even so, his eventual acceptance of
the situation showed great maturity.

But just as life can be cruel, it can also be strangely gratifying.
After Jonathan came out of his coma, his relationship with his
brother changed dramatically. As Jonathan gradually recovered, one
of the things he suffered from was memory loss. As far as his relationship with his brother went, this memory loss had unforeseen advantages. As Jonathan explained recently:

> One of the things that happens when you lose your memory is
> you lose your shtick. Family shtick, in this case. The weird thing
> is: my relationship with my brother is better than it has ever been.
> I don't view what he is saying to me through the prism of our

past. It's not coloured by our lifelong relationship. He'll call me up now just to shoot the breeze. Or to say, "Let's go to a movie." We've never done that kind of thing in our lives.

Jonathan's accident was not the first time he launched our family on an emotional rollercoaster ride. As I mentioned earlier, he was diagnosed with cancer – Hodgkin's – when he was twenty-one, the year he attended the London School of Economics. What I did not mention earlier was how much of an effect this diagnosis had on our family. Roz still believes Jonathan's illness changed our family irrevocably.

For me, it was a reminder that there are some things you cannot control, some problems that are beyond your power to solve. During that time, I was, in Jonathan's words, "a basket case." In fact, more than once I was told to refrain from visiting him in the hospital because I was not helping the situation.

Still, the prognosis for Hodgkin's was good. From the start, we knew that, in this particular instance, it was considered a curable disease. Still, after Jonathan received his chemotherapy treatment in Montreal, we went for a consultation to the Brigham and Women's Hospital in Boston (an affiliate of the renowned Dana-Farber Cancer Institute), and an intern there took one look at my concerned expression and said, "Why are you so worried? We cure these cases."

In stark contrast, Jonathan's bicycle accident, some twenty years later, was much more critical. It was life and death from the beginning and remained that way for what seemed like an excruciatingly long time. The reality of just how bleak things had been for Jonathan became clear after he emerged from his coma. On 4 October, Debbie was in from New York visiting her brother when he confided to her the terrifying doubts he had had about his recovery. He even confessed he was, for a time, not sure he wanted to recover. Debbie wrote about what Jonathan told her in an email to Roz:

> Today [Jonathan] told me that at one point he was deciding whether he should fight to recover or not. This must have been when he was first coming out of the coma. He was worried about his family and was not sure if it would be better for them if he were dead as opposed to being handicapped and thus becoming a lifelong burden to them. He said when someone dies you eventually get over it and can move on. If he lived and were a vegetable or a quadriplegic etc. ... he would make their lives

more difficult. He thought about it for a while and then decided he would fight to get better.

And he has fought and persevered. His recovery, all of us believe, is directly related to his fierce, heroic determination. It has been incredible for the whole family to see how hard he has pushed himself, how hard he has worked to get better. He has had to learn the most basic things all over again – from speaking to eating to walking. His sense of humour, however, has remained intact. For instance, Sacré-Coeur is a predominantly francophone hospital and Jonathan was forced to speak more French there than he ever had before. "I had to fall on my head," he joked to us, "to speak the French language."

After Jonathan was released from Sacré-Coeur, he went for a period of rehabilitation to the Institut Réadaptation Gingras-Lindsay de Montréal (IRGLM), a hospital with which I turned out to have a personal connection. The link was Uncle Dave, Dr. David Sherman, a gerontologist who was married to Anne Doner, Roz's mother's sister. Over the years, Uncle Dave and I had become very close. Beyond our dayjobs in the world of medicine, we share the same interests. We had the same views on world affairs; we both loved cantorial music and enjoyed singing. Most of all, we were both inquisitive men, interested in furthering our knowledge in whatever way we could.

Uncle Dave and Aunt Anne became surrogate grandparents to our children and we spent many Friday nights in their home. In fact, Dana and Jonathan named their youngest child Orly Anne after Aunt Anne, who had always been like a second mother to Roz. As for Uncle Dave, he was one of the most humble and decent men I have known, a man respected in his profession and by his colleagues.

Which is why, in 1962, when he came to ask me to help him and his employer, Dr, Gustave Gingras, with a project they were about to embark on, I was more than happy to oblige. This was shortly after Dr. Gingras, a pioneer in the field of rehabilitation in Quebec, had opened the IRGLM and appointed Uncle Dave his scientific director and chief medical researcher.

One of Gingras's most significant contributions was the work he did with Thalidomide survivors. In the 1950s and into the 1960s, Thalidomide was commonly prescribed to pregnant women to alleviate nausea. It proved to have tragic side effects, causing fetal birth defects in a number of cases. Babies were born missing limbs or with severely deformed limbs, often with flippers instead of arms or legs or both. Worse still, these babies, as they grew into children, were not able to use ordinary prosthetic devices. However, Dr. Gingras had heard about a prosthetic arm that was being developed by German scientists in Heidelberg, called the Heidelberg Arm, devised specifically for Thalidomide victims. It is worth noting that Thalidomide has been rehabilitated in recent years, becoming the drug of choice in treating multiple myeloma. Yet another example of how an old drug that failed terribly in its original usage has, thanks to the persistence of scientific inquiry as well as pharmaceutical research and development, become useful in its second incarnation.

In 1962, however, Dr. Gingras and Uncle Dave were dealing with Thalidomide's catastrophic consequences. They were determined to go to Germany to investigate the Heidelberg Arm and equally determined to bring it back to Canada. Uncle Dave asked me, as well as about a dozen other Montrealers, to help fund the purchase of the arm and I contributed $12,000 to the cause. In fact there was, as I was reminded when I visited Jonathan at the IRGLM, a plaque on the fourth floor for those of us who had participated in the fundraising effort. Here it was, almost fifty years later, and I was in a rehab hospital I had never dreamed I would be in again, visiting my son as he recovered from his nearly fatal accident, being shown a plaque with my name on it. I recalled, too, that I had designed the IRGLM's first pharmacy at Dr. Gingras's request. Life is, indeed, curious. Sometimes, you can even be forgiven for thinking, as the irrepressible Tevye says in *Fiddler on the Roof*, that God just might have a plan for everything and everyone.

Jonathan went from IRGLM to the Constance-Lethbridge Rehabilitation Centre in Montreal West for treatment, most recently as an outpatient. His team there – speech-language pathologist Michelle Bourque, physiotherapist Gabrielle Gaudreault-Malépart, neuropsychologist Hélène Cabonneau, kinesiologist Marc Bétournay, occupational therapist Amélie Labelle, social worker and case manager Andréanne Roy, and Dr. Debrah White – have all been exceptional.

Indeed, the care he has received from all these institutions has been consistently outstanding, prompting Roz to write a letter to the editorial section of the *Montreal Gazette*. Under the heading "Medicare: a Good Reason to Pay Taxes," the letter lauded the sometimes maligned health care system in our city, our province, and our country. Roz chronicled, in some detail, the care Jonathan received at the Sacré-Coeur trauma unit, the ICU, and on the ward, adding:

There is a lot of criticism of our medical system. It is not perfect. But without medicare, the cost of this world-class care could bankrupt any middle-income family. We are so fortunate to live in this wonderful country. Paying taxes is a great privilege!

In fact, in gratitude to the team at the Sacré-Coeur that treated Jonathan, Jonathan, along with his brother and sisters and their families, funded a room, a bedroom really, for the families of patients of the trauma centre, especially for those who were from out of town. The idea was to make sure they would have a place to stay so they could be close to their loved one for what would often be extended periods.

For a long time, Jonathan never thought he would go back to work at Paladin, the company he had built into a huge success. Throughout his recovery process, he has been hard on himself. Initially, he was convinced going back to Paladin was not in his future. As he put it not long ago: "I ran a public company. I have brain damage. I don't think that can be done."

At first, he was content to walk his son, Noah, to school every day and he was keeping busy, a little too busy perhaps, making plans to keep up his charity work, especially on behalf of Jewish education. But, as we learned from the day of the accident, it was a mistake to underestimate him. Indeed, every day how remarkable his recovery is becomes more and more evident. There is still a long way to go and a lot of obstacles to overcome, but I have no doubt he can overcome them. What would turn out to be the last entry in his mother's journal, dated January 2012, five months after the accident, provides an accurate description of his and our family's long journey:

> It is only a matter of one day and ... everything familiar is gone and a new reality settles in ... When I think about it now I understand that the miracle that happened to us took place in the... prayers that were being said all over the world for Jonathan. When a community is united around something, it simply happens. We realized how blessed we were to have our whole community behind us.
>
> For the first sixteen days most doctors had lost hope but we didn't ... At this point in Jonathan's recovery ... he is a walking miracle!

This has been a difficult chapter to write and not one I expected to have to write. Jonathan's accident occurred while I was in the middle of telling the story of a life that has, in large part, run smoothly; that has been, in many ways, remarkably fortunate. But my son's hard road to recovery, hard as it has been for all of us, especially him, has served to bring our family closer together than ever. It has also reminded me of what the first Israeli president, David Ben-Gurion, once said: "Anyone who doesn't believe in miracles is not a realist."

Epilogue

One's life must matter.
Margaret Thatcher from *The Iron Lady*

I have worked hard and I have been lucky. These two facts of my life have always been inextricably intertwined. And writing this book has made this realization clearer to me than ever. At the same time that I have been fortunate to have always been involved in a business I love; I have laboured fervently to balance the work I do with my commitment to my family and my community.

Writing *To Make a Difference* has also provided me with a rare opportunity to reflect on a long and happy life, one filled with challenges, certainly – with all those "hills to climb" – but also with its fair share of successes. Still, I am keenly aware that looking back has never really been my natural inclination. As this book demonstrates, I am a man who has always been intent on looking forward. Finally, the time has come to do just that.

The businesses I have begun or have been an integral part of in my sixty years in the pharmaceutical industry – from Winley-Morris to ICN Canada to Pharmascience – have always been imbued with the same theme: improvement. From the start, I have remained dedicated to developing drugs and treatments that are more easily available, more affordable, and, simply put, better. Making lives better has been a constant principle in my decision to sell pharmaceuticals.

I am also very proud of the fact that Pharmscience is a "mini United Nations," employing people from every corner of the world.

Pharmascience's position as a private, family business has also been a principle I have tried my best to maintain. It has not always been easy and I have no illusions that it will not continue to be difficult in the future. And while I know that there are companies in Europe that have been owned by families – though often run by professional management – for over 400 years, I also know these kinds of businesses can destroy families. It is my hope, then, that Pharmascience will help to hold our family together in the future. Still, if it is not able to do so, I would hope that it would be sold. I never want it to be a cause of grief or division in the lives of my grandchildren or their children.

And while *To Make a Difference* is written with an enduring faith in the future of my family, it is also written with some concern for what that future might hold. Roz and I are confident our children, Deborah, David, Jonathan, and Shawna, have absorbed the lessons of compassion and caring we have set out to teach them. We could hardly feel otherwise. After all, we have seen them put those lessons into practice in their daily lives. We have seen them build strong families with strong partners; we have seen them make a significant mark in their respective communities. In addition, I have been a proud witness as each of them, in turn, has sought out and found meaningful careers, careers they love.

But writing *To Make a Difference* has also served to remind me that the world is a much different place than the world in which I or even my children grew up and came-of-age. As a consequence, the readers that I am most intent on reaching with this book are my grandchildren and their children.

And it is written with the full understanding that this audience may prove to be a hard one to reach. I can only assume that future generations of the Goodman, Sone, and Davis families, and, hopefully, other families, too, will have both the opportunity and the desire to read *To Make a Difference*. I also recognize that this is, in our high-speed, internet, smart phone, iPad, Facebook, distraction-filled age, a rather large and optimistic assumption. For all I know, reading will be obsolete in the not too distant future.

As for the challenges future generations will face – the hills they will need the strength to climb – I hope that this book, if and when they do come across it, will convey that the lessons I learned in my life are unlikely to be altered by new technologies and trends.

By nature, I am an optimist. I believe in the potential to make the world a better place and make one's self a better person. And I am most profoundly optimistic that, given the examples set out in this book as well as the examples set by their parents, my grandchildren, their children, and all future generations will see that the important things – family, community, a meaningful occupation, and the desire to help others – will never go out of fashion. I sincerely hope that whatever economic independence they may be lucky enough to have does not deter them from finding creative challenges that will enrich their lives and help them find the same sense of fulfillment I have.

We are, in the end, custodians for the generations to come. We are compelled to protect our resources, our ideals, our values in order to help build a better world for our grandchildren and, in turn, for their children. I still believe, as I always have, that we can teach best by example, by our mistakes as well as our successes. This book is a chronicle of both. It is a testament to the moments, the people, and the events that have mattered most in my life. But it is also meant to be something more – a challenge to everyone to go on making a difference.

8 December 2013

Acknowledgments

I learned from writing *To Make a Difference* that a book, even the most personal one, is a collaborative effort. My thanks, therefore, go to everyone at McGill-Queen's University Press who offered their guidance in readying the manuscript for publication. My thanks, too, go to the late Joe King, a stalwart chronicler of Jewish Montreal, for his help with this book when it was in its earliest stages. I am especially indebted to Sam Altman, Robin Mader, Gary Munden, and Stanley Plotnick for the insight and diligent attention they brought to early versions of the manuscript.

Although in *To Make a Difference* I concentrate on the people involved in the very early startup of Pharmascience, I would be remiss if I did not mention the contribution made to the company's success by the employees of Pharmel, our first production site. They include Maurice Meloche, Pharmel's president, from whom I bought the company, Jacques Beaulieu, Pharmel's production manager, Nancy Hatfield, who managed packaging, and Wolfgang Ritter, who ran quality control.

I am also grateful for the loyalty of the pharmacists and pharmacy chains who have, year by year, increased their purchases. I am indebted, as well, to all our partners around the world who have been major contributors to our success.

It is impossible, of course, to mention all the Pharmascience employees – some 1,300 currently – who are a vital part of the company's evolution. While the stories in this book pinpoint special events in the growth of Pharmascience, I am deeply grateful for the way in which our research and development team, under the management of scientific director Dr. Len Neirinck, created so many new generic products. These products were then expertly introduced into the Canadian market by teams led by Debby Ship and Sam Galet.

Other long-time employees have helped, in immeasurable ways, to make Pharmascience the success it is today. They include Marc Beaulieu, Carole Béchard, Lucie Bélanger, Robert Bérubé, Claudette Blais-Beck, Daniel Bouchard, Guy Boucher, Janet Boys, Mario Brochu, Yves Chaput, Mercella Colquhoun, Dale Conway, Michael Cooke, Jocelyne Couture, Loida David, Rolando Deblois, Eric Delisle, Jacqueline Digenova, Shelley Donnelly, Suzanne Dubé, Denis Ducap, Claudette Dulude, Aladino Feniza, Wendy Flynn, Guylaine Fortin, Hélène Fournier, Rihab Francis, Barry Gagne, Gaetano Gallo, Claude Garceau, Neil Goodbrand, Claude Girard, Lise Girard, Yves Grenier, Nathalie Guay, Michel Guillemette, Leocardy Joseph, Yasmine Kadri, Edouard Karib, Catherine Kelly-Hoefman, Sylvie Labelle, Claudette Labrecque, Marc Lacasse, Nicole Langlois, Guillaume Laporte, Suzanne Laporte, Daniel Lavoie, Yvonne Layne, Louise Lortie, Ginette Major, Nicole Marchand, Christopher Melrose, Nicole McLean, Joseph David Meaney, Carole Mercier, Kharoonah Mohit, Claire Montgomery, Jo'Anne Myre, Alain Nelson, Nicole Neveu, Kenny New, Thai Nhu Nguyen, Francoise Ouellet, Ginette Paquet, Anne-Marie Paquette, Chhibu Patel, Keith Paul, Francine Pépin, Florence Poulin, Dominique Pouliot, Louise Proulx, Claudette Proulx-Beck, Alain Provost, Celine Racine, Mala M. Ratnadurai, Sylvain Richer, Juliette Rivest, Serge Roch, Robert Roussin, Crisanto M. Salazar, Gilda Shahin-Abdulezer, Margot Swan, Jocelyne Tessier, Claudette Thomas, Barbara Touchette, Diane Trudeau, Carole Vezina, Jean Roger Victor, Steven A. Williams, Jocelyne Wolff, Nader Zibazadeh.